Kingdom Come

Ministry Principles and Priorities

Doug Newton

Mary's Place Publishing
Bowling Green, Kentucky

Kingdom Come
©2009 by Doug Newton

Published by Mary's Place Publishing
571 Stump Bluff Rd.
Bowling Green, KY 42101

Printed in the United States of America

ISBN 0-9748257-5-1

All rights reserved. No part of this publication may be used or reproduced in any manner whatsoever, stored in a retrieval system, or transmitted in any form or by any means—for example, electronic, photocopy, recording— without prior written permission. The only exception is brief quotations in printed reviews.

All scripture quotations, unless otherwise indicated, are taken from the HOLY BIBLE, NEW INTERNATIONAL VERSION®. NIV®. Copyright ©1973, 1978, 1984 by International Bible Society. Used by permission of Zondervan. All rights reserved.

*For the people
and the future of
Greenville Free Methodist Church.*

*For maximum impact
on our community and our world.*

For the glory of God.

more than a vision.

Every church needs **a vision**. But even a common vision doesn't go far enough these days. The question is how do you get there? That's where things get dicey. The world is complicated. It takes sophisticated GPS guidance in more ways than just travel to help us navigate. Even with a clear vision a church can still get bogged down in 101 different paths and priorities. There's got to be **a common method**. Not only that, people with a common vision can pursue that vision for different reasons. If that happens, some day in the future there will be trouble… "I thought we were focusing on outreach to increase our attendance, not start all these programs that drain our budget!" You see, there's got to be **a common passion**, too. Turns out there's a lot more than just vision to this matter of being a church that goes somewhere. That's what this book is about. It's a working plan for how our church can move with a common passion taking up **a common challenge** based on a common hope. You'll see an overview of it all on the next four pages. It looks and works like a table of contents. Then the succeeding pages provide more detailed explanations. So sharpen your No.2 pencil. It will be on the quiz.

Overview

6 OUR PASSION
GOD'S KINGDOM.
To see God's Kingdom come and people set free and transformed.

8 OUR VISION
MAXIMUM IMPACT.
We will have maximum impact on our community as a true "house of prayer."

- 10 a "crowd mentality"
- 12 a true house of prayer
- 14 rescue and restoration
- 16 focus on poverty

18 OUR METHOD
KINGDOM-TEACHING.
We are a kingdom-teaching church.

To teach the Kingdom, we:
- 20 seek its coming
- 21 define its nature
- 24 clarify its dimensions
- 26 overcome its foes
- 29 practice its ways

30 OUR EMPHASES
TRUTH. FREEDOM. TRANSFORMATION.
Ten emphases we promote:

- 32 The performative nature of God's Word.
- 33 The priority of prayer in the Spirit.
- 34 The importance of proclamation.
- 35 Persuasive demonstrations of the Spirit.
- 36 The full scope of salvation.
- 37 Entire sanctification as crisis and process.
- 38 Spiritual warfare and steps to freedom.
- 39 The "greater" Great Commission.
- 40 *Situational* spiritual gifts.
- 41 Six character traits of radical discipleship.

42 OUR CHALLENGE
ERADICATE POVERTY.

*To live kingdom principles so fully and effectively that we see **the eradication of all forms of poverty in our community in 20 years.***

44 What do we mean by "poverty"?
45 What do we mean by "eradicate"?
46 Is it doable?

If we are to fulfill our collective challenge, we must focus on a four-fold plan:

48 Seek Spirit-provided gifts of service.
49 Free up Big Money.
50 Employ "substitutionary debt payment."
51 Facilitate a good system.

The heart of the plan is to inspire each family to rescue one family every 2-3 years.

52 OUR HOPE
GOD'S NATURE.

Our vision for maximum impact is based on God's nature being love and His stated will for the salvation of the whole world. We are convinced that God is honored and pleased as we set our sights on having **maximum impact.**

56 OUR DISCIPLESHIP GOAL
EXPERIENCE. EXTEND.

To produce fully-devoted followers of Jesus Christ who:
*embrace **truth**,*
*enter **freedom**,*
*and experience **transformation***

and then extend truth, freedom and transformation to a needy world.

58 OUR VENUES
PURPOSEFUL FOCUS.

LARGE GROUP GATHERINGS

to evangelize seekers.
Mode: Proclamation
Desired result: hearts opened with vision, hope and response
Movement direction: Seeker to believer

MID-SIZE CLASSES

to edify believers.
Mode: Instruction
Desired result: minds shaped by faith, knowledge and commitment
Movement direction: Believer to follower

SMALL GROUPS

to equip followers.
Mode: Application
Desired result: wills trained with love, skills and tasks
Movement direction: Follower to transformer

62 OUR PROVISION
RESTFUL WORK.

Those who join Jesus in Kingdom work find rest and reward.

66 SOME EXTRAS

66   **APPENDIX A:** How Saved Can You Get?

70   **APPENDIX B:** Healing Today?

76   **APPENDIX C:** Behind the Closed Door

Our Passion: God's Kingdom

To see God's Kingdom come and people set free and transformed!

When it comes to having a passion, can any church go wrong combining Jesus' personal mission with the very first request in the Lord's prayer? In that prayer Jesus urged His followers to say *May Your kingdom come* and Your will be done on earth as it is in heaven.[1] He had just gotten finished telling them not to pursue anything—not even food, clothing or shelter—more than they *seek the kingdom of God*.[2] Soon after, He sent out His disciples with one lead message that He called the "gospel": *The kingdom of God is at hand!*[3] Then when He taught, His topic in stories, parables and plain language was almost always about *the kingdom of God*.[4] This was His singular emphasis. And so it makes perfect sense to interpret His personal mission statement as a good description of the purpose and results of the kingdom of God on earth: *The Spirit of the Lord... has anointed me to preach good news to the poor. He has sent me to proclaim freedom for the prisoners and recovery of sight for the blind, to release the oppressed..."*[5]

[1] Matthew 6:10   [2] Matthew 6:33   [3] Matthew 10:7   [4] Matthew 13:24, 31, 33   [5] Luke 4:18

Often this description is thought to be about four different categories of human suffering: *poverty, blindness, imprisonment* and *oppression*. But in actuality all of the human problems found in this passage that Jesus was quoting from Isaiah[6] occurred because people were in bondage to an oppressive power. Even the problem of blindness was not caused by some lack of physical capability, but rather from being in the pitch black darkness of a prison cell. Therefore "recovery of sight" meant being brought out of the darkness of prison into the daylight of freedom.

In a nutshell, the coming of the kingdom of God means **freedom** from all forms of bondage. That bondage can involve physical suffering, emotional anguish or mental confusion, financial problems, dysfunctional relationships, destructive addictions and spiritual unrest.

Regardless of the exact nature of the problem, there is always some degree of satanic interference that must be eliminated in order for the problem to be effectively addressed. That's why Jesus focused His attacks on this ultimate enemy: *The reason the Son of God appeared was to destroy the devil's work.*[7]

The nature of human bondage, its scope and severity, fuels our compassion for people and our passion for the coming of God's kingdom in its full power and expression, so that we can carry on the same works Jesus performed.[8]

But should any church expect to see the same results from the coming of God's kingdom today? Didn't all those powerful signs and wonders during Jesus' ministry and the early church occur simply as evidence to support the gospel message?

No. Signs and wonders are not just *evidence* of the kingdom; they are the *essence* of the bondage-breaking kingdom. Wherever God's authority is enforced, the enemy's strongholds, tactics and deceits are exposed and deposed.[9] Then and only then can people be transformed.

Freedom must come before transformation. For too long the Christian church has called people to live godly lives without breaking the powers that hold them in sin and sickness. It's like expecting a person in chains to run a race. Jesus accused the religious establishment of His day of this very cruelty. *You load people down with burdens they can hardly carry, and you yourselves will not lift one finger to help them.*[10]

If we want people to live holy, transformed lives we must "help them" by making effective freedom ministries our top priority, and kingdom presence and power our primary pursuit.

If we pursue this passion something amazing will happen to us and to our community.

Turn the page to begin seeing what's possible and how it can come about.

---

[6] Isaiah 61:1-2; 58:6   [7] 1 John 3:8   [8] John 14:12   [9] 2 Corinthians 2:11, 10:4-5; Ephesians 6:10-22; Colossians 2:15   [10] Luke 11:46

OUR Vision: MAXImum imPACT

We will have maximum impact on our community as a true house of prayer.

God's plan of salvation is focused on the whole world. Yes, He loves you and me as individuals. But it was because He so loved the **whole world**[1] that He gave His only Son Jesus to live among us, die on the cross, rise from the dead, and empower the church.

The *global-sized dimensions* of human need *require God-sized actions*.

No church is truly passionate about the kingdom of God without setting its sight on having **maximum impact**. Random acts of kindness won't cut it. Only **strategic acts of rescue** will do in a world where 25,000 children die daily for lack of clean water. Or where an estimated 1 out of every 5 girls is sexually abused by the time she is 16.

Only the saving work of God through faith in Jesus Christ will transform people and cultures. But that means massive numbers of people must hear about, see evidence and believe in the power of God.

[1] John 3:16

So simply put, by **maximum impact** we mean: *As many people as possible having as much evidence as necessary to come to faith and wholeness in Jesus Christ.*

At first glance, the idea of maximum impact may sound like we are concerned about attracting large numbers of people and growing a large church. Exactly!

Jesus is our model in that regard. It's impossible to read the historical accounts of Jesus' public ministry and miss the fact that He attracted large crowds of people. That seemed to be His starting point. Now, some people argue that the crowds were very fickle. They were here today and gone tomorrow. True. Does that mean large group ministry was a strategic error?

Let's examine this issue a little farther. Because, if our vision is maximum impact we need to settle this matter of whether it's right to target "as many people as possible."

As many people as possible having as much evidence as necessary to come to faith and wholeness in Jesus Christ.

A Crowd Mentality

Most people find crowds stimulating! Something about singing the Star Spangled Banner with 35,000 people in a stadium gives goose bumps unlike sitting at home watching on TV. Large crowds seem to enhance experiences.

Interestingly, large churches with big crowds are ridiculed by many Christians these days. They get accused of shallowness. But perhaps we should rethink our prejudice against "large" crowd-oriented ministry.

Did you know there are 122 references in the gospels to Jesus ministering directly to large crowds?

In 16 of 22 chapters in Matthew prior to His last week Jesus is relating directly to large crowds. Put all the gospels together. Out of 65 chapters prior to the crucifixion narratives, Jesus is relating directly to large crowds in 41 of them. That's a whopping 63%!

The common perception is that Jesus' priority method of ministry was to "small groups"—focusing on His twelve disciples most of the time. The previous observations in the biblical text call this claim into question.

His "crowd ministry" was characterized by

extensive teaching and **widespread healing** that left people amazed. Two verses capture this two-fold "crowd" ministry of Jesus.

> *Jesus then left that place and went into the region of Judea and across the Jordan. Again crowds of people came to him, and as was his custom,* ***he taught them***. [1]

> *Yet the news about him spread all the more, so that crowds of people came to hear him and* ***to be healed of their sicknesses***. [2]

And what's more: most all of His recorded teaching and miracles happened in the context of crowds, not small groups.

So we should not be thinking that one is more important than the other. Small groups or large groups. Each is important, and one should not be emphasized to the neglect of the other.

To underscore this point ask yourself: were the crowds of people that flocked to Jesus a surprise to Him? Did He react, "Oops! I had no idea people would start flocking to me"?

No, of course not. If attracting large crowds is what happened, then that is what He wanted to happen. It was part of His plan.

Large group ministry was where He cracked open people's minds and inspired their hearts with hope. It was the place He described what the kingdom of God was like, and showed them how open it was and how close at hand it had come. It was the place He proved the presence of the kingdom by demonstrations of delivering and healing power. Not just for a lucky few, but for everyone who came to Him. Everyone! Unlike any other venue, crowds were where He illustrated that most basic spirit of the kingdom: *whoever will may come*.[3]

That's the kingdom: the outpouring of God's delivering power and healing grace. That's what He wanted crowds of people to see! Not just His close insiders. In fact, the small groups were for training disciples so that even larger groups could be served.

Jesus wants crowds!

So what does that mean to us? That means we must also want to attract and minister to crowds. It also means we *don't* ask: what can our church become if we seek God's kingdom first and obey the Lord? Rather we think big. We adopt a crowd mentality. We ask:

What can our community become if the people of our church seek God's kingdom first and obey the Lord?

Our vision is about our world, not ourselves.

Turn to the next page to discover where we focus all our energies in order to have this kind of maximum impact.

---

[1] Mark 10:1   [2] Luke 5:15   [3] Acts 2:21; Revelation 22:17; 2 Peter 3:9

True House of Prayer

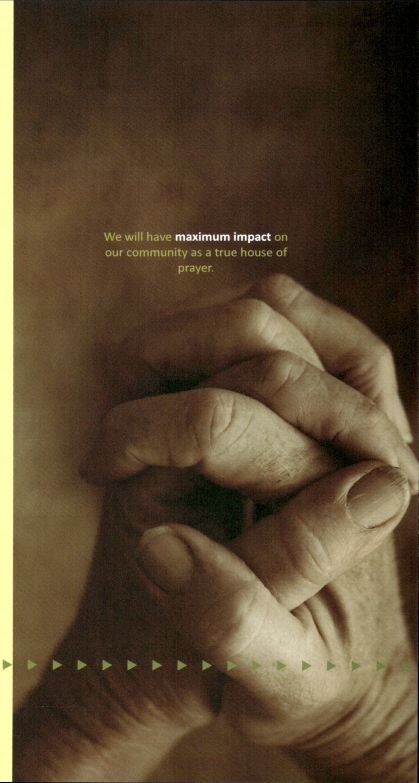

We will have **maximum impact** on our community as a true house of prayer.

The only act of "violence" Jesus ever committed was to drive a bunch of profiteers out of the temple in Jerusalem. Most likely He never actually hit anyone. But that's small consolation to those who were certainly traumatized by this man overturning tables and snapping a whip to chase them away. Needless to say, His passion should command our attention. Why did He blow up at these people? ▶ ▶ ▶ ▶ ▶

The words He shouted tell the whole story:

"It is written," he said to them, " 'My house will be called a house of prayer,' but you are making it a 'den of robbers.' " [1]

Interestingly, in His righteous anger He was actually quoting scripture!—the prophet Isaiah. What was Isaiah talking about?

First, compare the portion of words Jesus quoted to God's full statement from Isaiah.

These I will bring to my holy mountain
 and give them joy in my house of prayer.
Their burnt offerings and sacrifices
 will be accepted on my altar;
for my house will be called
 a house of prayer for all nations. [2]

This prophecy talks about God bringing certain people to His "holy mountain" and giving them joy in His "house of prayer." Who are these people? This prophecy refers in general to foreigners—people who formerly had been excluded from gaining access to the mercies of God—and broken people. Specifically eunuchs.

A eunuch was a man who was castrated. He had his manhood taken away. Originally, when God was establishing the people of Israel as a nation, He set down explicit instructions to exclude eunuchs from entering the assembly of the Lord.

No one who has been emasculated by crushing or cutting may enter the assembly of the LORD. [3]

A high premium was placed on cleanness and wholeness in order to come before God.

Now the prophet Isaiah declares that when salvation and righteousness is revealed[4] (a clear reference to the coming Messiah) the doors of acceptance would be thrown open not just to include eunuchs (representing those who are not whole), but to bless them with "full restoration" to a life better than before their brokenness.

To them I will give within my temple walls
a memorial and a name better than sons and daughters; I will give them an everlasting name that will not be cut off. [5]

Perhaps surprisingly, the idea of the "house of prayer" is not so much focused on the activity of prayer per se, as it is focused on who gets to be welcomed within the embrace of God's saving grace and blessing. And the scope is global!

Those who once used to be excluded due to their unacceptability will now be acceptable and included. And the temple is the place—the "house of prayer"—where that introduction and inclusion in the saving grace of God will be experienced.

This is a powerful promise for all broken people that is richly illustrated in the case of the eunuch and then emphatically reinforced at the very beginning of the Christian era. Who do you think was the very first identified convert to Christianity once the gospel spread beyond Jewish

---

[1] Matthew 21:13   [2] Isaiah 56:7   [3] Deuteronomy 23:1   [4] Isaiah 56:1   [5] Isaiah 56:5

Jerusalem to the uttermost parts of the non-Jewish world? An Ethiopian eunuch.[1]

This wasn't a coincidence. Philip, the evangelist, was given explicit instructions by an angel that led him directly to the eunuch[2] who was reading (coincidentally?) Isaiah the prophet. You see, God Himself never fails to keep His Word. In fact, He promised, *I am watching to see that my word is fulfilled.*[3]

So to sum it up, the **house of prayer** is supposed to be a place where:

- *excluded and **broken people are welcomed** within the embrace of God's saving grace,*
- *saving grace is a matter of **full restoration**, and*
- *prayer means the hope of full restoration for people of all nations.*

So when Jesus walked in and saw the business of religion ironically squeezing out room for the ministry of inclusion and full restoration, He got angry.

Then He accused them of turning His house into a *den of robbers*. Literally, a haven for *anti-government guerillas.*[4]

Can it be any clearer? If we have a passion for the kingdom of God, we must have a vision for maximum impact by being a true house of prayer that draws crowds and brings complete restoration to anyone and everyone everywhere.

[1] Acts 8:26-39   [2] Acts 8: 26, 29   [3] Jeremiah 1:12   [4] Jewish historian Josephus   [5] Luke 19:10   [6] Psalm 103:3-4

Rescue and Restoration • • •

If Jesus' "cleansing of the temple" tirade reveals anything, it shows that He is absolutely determined that prayer should remain at the very center of His kingdom.

Now that we have seen the "house of prayer" term in its biblical context, we also have a clearer idea of what Jesus meant by prayer and what He was promoting.

Prayer is often about connecting with God not so much for your sake but the sake of others. The term "seeking God's face" in prayer often means discovering where He is looking. His face—and heart—is riveted on people who need to be rescued.

We serve a God who seeks the lost,[5] **who binds up the broken hearted, who lifts people out of the pit, who hears their cries and heals their diseases.**[6] In short, He looks for people to rescue.

When Jesus clarified what it meant to love God

and love your neighbor, it was no accident that He told a story of rescue.[7] The main character in this parable known as the *good Samaritan* stands for all time as our model of rescue ***and*** restoration. We should go and do likewise.[8]

That means we live our lives on alert. We keep our eyes peeled. Ready to rescue.

The ministry of rescue and restoration is a far cry from today's mantra of doing *random acts of kindness.*

The bruised and beaten man found alongside the road was not going to be helped by a mere bottle of water. Or a handout at Thanksgiving. He needed emergency help from someone who would place him under watchful and resourceful care ***until he was fully restored***. That was Jesus' illustration of loving your neighbor.

Funny how His illustration of loving your neighbor and the description of the "house of prayer" as a place of total restoration mesh so well.

No wonder Jesus was so adamant that His temple be preserved as a "house of prayer."

This is what it will take to have maximum impact.

Since it is now the case that each individual Christian is a temple of the Holy Spirit[9], we each must become a place of heart-changing and **RESCUING PRAYER.** How else could anyone hope to have a heart compassionate enough and abilities competent enough to do over and over again what the good Samaritan did that one time.

But here's the deal. Once any Christian really sells out to this lifestyle of being poised for rescue and restoration, you start getting more radical about the big societal problems that keep crushing people and holding them in bondage.

For example, take the case of the good Samaritan

---

[7] Luke 10:30ff   [8] Luke 10:37   [9] 1 Corinthians 3:16, 6:19

again. The man he rescued was beaten by robbers and left for dead. This road to Jerusalem was a dangerous road. What if the next day the Samaritan found another beaten man alongside the road? And the next day another?

At some point the Samaritan is going to run out of money and time to rescue anyone else. So he's got to think of another plan. A more systemic plan of rescue. How about one that rescues people before they get robbed and beaten? If this were a modern story, he would undoubtedly think about streetlights. Ah, there's rescue before the fact!

In the same way, it is impossible to be moved by God's compassion for broken people without thinking about the big social problems that batter their lives.

Suddenly, we aren't talking about emergency aid. Now we're talking about societal transformation. And there's no better place to start than with the problem of poverty—the most dangerous and destructive road any person can travel.

Focus on Poverty

Anyone who begins to look out at the world of human need with the eyes and heart of God can't help but see the devastation of poverty in all its forms. Lack of jobs, education, medical care, transportation and opportunity result in broken homes and beleaguered people. Vicious cycles of crime, addictions and abuse spawn succeeding generations of brokenness and hopelessness.

Poverty must be addressed.

Unfortunately, all too often the typical church tends to "spiritualize" key biblical mandates about poverty by talking mostly about spiritual poverty as the real problem that needs to be addressed.

However, if we take our cues from God, we cannot fail to focus on material poverty. Our God is so commited to the needs of the economically poor and socially disenfranchised that He created economic and social systems for His people that were

designed to lift the poor out of poverty and give them a fresh start.

The most massive system was the *Jubilee* system. Under this system financial debts were literally wiped clean every seven years. Apparently God understands impoverished people can get so far behind that they will never catch up. But who would ever loan money if they knew the debt would be erased in seven years?

God called that attitude "wicked."

> *Be careful not to harbor this wicked thought: "The seventh year, the year for canceling debts, is near," so that you do not show ill will toward your needy brother and give him nothing.*[1]

You see the spirit He wants us to have toward the poor? We are supposed to show so much compassion that people who have fallen on hard times—regardless of the reason—will be restored and given a good chance for a different life.

But this spirit is not to be applied only on a case by case basis. God's program was designed not only to lift up individuals and families, but the whole society. Under the Jubilee system, on every 50th year the balance of wealth was reset. Land that was lost through adverse circumstances was returned to the original owner.[2]

This was a radical economic system that favored rescue for those who were knocked down by life circumstances for whatever reason.

The bottom line: Our God decrees flatly, "There shall be no poor among you."[3]

In case anyone would argue that these were rescue and restoration systems designed only for ancient times, we point out that this same spirit was clearly infused into the early church at its very beginning on a day now known as Pentecost. According to historical records early Christians freely sold their possessions, like houses and land, and gave the proceeds to make sure there were no needy persons among them.[4]

So you see, wherever God comes—that is to say, wherever His Kingdom comes—He brings this spirit of a no-holds-barred commitment to rescue the poor. One by one. And in society as a whole.

In fact, this is of such concern that the only capital crime recorded in the New Testament was committed by two people who conspired to fake compassion to the poor![5]

• • • • • • • • • • • • • • •

To sum up this whole section on vision: we believe *maximum impact involves great crowds of people coming to faith and wholeness because we have committed ourselves to being a true house of prayer—a place of rescue and restoration—with a special emphasis on the broken and poor.*

Of course it's one thing to have a vision, it's another to have an effective method. That's where we head next.

---

[1] Deuteronomy 15:9   [2] Leviticus 25:8ff   [3] Deuteronomy 15:4-5   [4] Acts 4:34-35   [5] Acts 5:1ff

OUR Method: kINGdom tEACHing

We believe our church is especially called and equipped to *teach* the Kingdom of God. But please pay attention to what we mean by teaching. Here's what the dictionary says:

> **Teach** (*tēch*) *vt. basic sense: "to show, demonstrate"* **1** to show or help a person to learn how to do something; **2** to give lessons to a pupil or class; **3** to help someone to develop a skill or trait; **4** to provide a person with knowledge or insight

To "teach the kingdom of God" does not mean to simply lecture or impart facts and information. A true teacher imparts knowledge and demonstrates skills that enable the student to become proficient and productive in a vocation.

That's what Jesus did. In fact, His followers called Him "Rabbi"—which means "teacher." Yes, He lectured. But much more than that, He modeled His lessons visually. He gave His disciples opportunities to practice through hands-on experience.

A teacher's goal is to pass on to students everything he or she knows and does, so that the students can do the very same things— maybe even better.

> Jesus said, "I tell you the truth, anyone who has faith in me will do what I have been doing. He will do even greater things than these..." [1]

When we say we are a kingdom-teaching church, we mean that we are raised up to do exactly what Jesus did as a teacher: show people what the Kingdom of God is like and how to live in its presence and according to its principles and power.

In a real sense, our method of kingdom teaching is just like teaching a teenager to drive. You don't instruct in a classroom. You take the keys of a multi-thousand dollar vehicle and hand them to a completely inexperienced novice who learns by doing what he or she does not yet know how to do. Hopefully, under the watchful guidance of an experienced driver.

This is our method—to hand over the keys of the kindgom. Obviously, that means we have to drive well ourselves. Meaning this: We must each know, experience and practice the ways of the kingdom.

The next few pages describe how that knowledge and experience comes about.

[1] John 14:12

seek ITS coming

You would think that a king would do whatever He pleased. That He would bring about whatever He wanted. Whenever He wanted to.

But when it comes to God's kingdom coming to earth, even though He desperately wants to bring it here, He often waits for us to seek it.

Jesus taught us to pray for its coming.[1] He said that seeking His kingdom must be of greater importance than the desire for food, shelter and clothing.[2]

Therefore, **teaching God's kingdom begins with teaching people how to seek.**

Interestingly, seeking is one of those things everybody knows how to do. Just think how passionate someone can be about finding lost money. Everything else is put on hold. You don't answer the phone. You don't do e-mail. You even put off eating. *Where's that money?!*

We all know how to seek. Now—can we seek the right thing? That's the question.

Fact is, most people's days are filled with energy and focus directed toward everything but God's kingdom coming. No doubt there are lots of things that compel our attention, that draw our focus away from the kingdom of God. It's understandable. But still, not excusable.

That's why the very first command that Jesus gave every time He announced the immediacy of the kingdom was to *repent*.[3]

The word repent means to make a 180° turnaround. That's what passionate seeking requires: ruthlessly resisting every object of concern that preoccupies your attention and causes you to neglect minute by minute involvement in God's kingdom.

As a church with a passion for God's kingdom, a vision for maximum impact, and a method of kingdom teaching, we must routinely prioritize times for repentance.

According to scripture, the Holy Spirit is responsible for bringing people to a place of personal conviction.[4] So we depend on Him to engender **a spirit of repentance.**

However, we must give Him time to do that work. People do not like to be told when they are wrong, particularly in our modern culture. Nevertheless, we must be committed

[1] Matthew 6:10 [2] Matthew 6:33 [3] Matthew 4:17 [4] John 16:8

Our Method: Kingdom Teaching

to create occasions for personal examination. We must take time in worship services and other venues to face our divided hearts and confess our sins. Consequently, our worship services must be open-ended if need be.

Also, seeking God's kingdom must be a corporate matter. We must do it together. As one body. While sheer numbers do not necessarily "move" God to action, there is biblical evidence that God pays attention to the heart of a collective group expressed through the unity of the majority of the people.[5]

Therefore, it is vitally important for as many people as possible to gather in agreement to seek God's kingdom.

This is a main reason we must place the highest priority on our ***corporate prayer gathering***. Just as nothing else should compete for our attention over the kingdom of God, we believe nothing should be allowed to compete with the prayer gatherings.

Define its Nature

People have all sorts of ideas about the kingdom of God. So if we are going to get serious about seeking its coming, we ought to get specific about its nature. Traditionally it is often said that the kingdom of God simply means the "rule of God." Therefore, to seek the kingdom simply means to seek the rule of God on earth and in your life. Consequently, most people see the "rule of God" primarily as a matter of following His moral laws and His divine will for your life. That's all well and good. But it falls short. How so?

The emphasis on moral righteousness is vital and requires the infilling of God's *supernatural character*, but it leaves out the other supernatural aspect of the kingdom—*supernatural ministry*.

This is a huge problem, because Jesus didn't come to earth just to make believers morally pure. He came to redeem the whole world, which requires ministry power.

For too many Christians, doing the miraculous works of the kingdom isn't even on their radar. All they

[5] Matthew 18:19; Acts 1:14-15, 2:1

DEFINE ITS NATURE (cont.)

think about is seeking the morality of the kingdom. In other words, it is possible to be seeking the kingdom of God passionately but miss it completely, because you're not open to or expecting all that the coming kingdom brings.

This was exactly the problem of the Pharisees, the religious people of Jesus' day. They fervently sought the moral dimensions of the kingdom. But when Jesus came healing the sick, delivering the demonized and serving the unclean they completely missed the kingdom.

Ironically, they were blind and deaf to the presence of the kingdom as Jesus healed the blind and deaf.

The same happens today to Christians who seek only the moral power of the kingdom and not the ministry power.

In one powerful episode Jesus permanently settled the question over the nature of the kingdom.

John the Baptist was the first to announce the kingdom of God and point to Jesus as the Messiah. But a few months down the road, he found himself in prison. He did not expect this, since he assumed that Jesus would establish God's kingdom and do away with the secular authorities.

So, somewhat confused and questioning, he sent some of his disciples to go ask Jesus if He really was the Messiah. After all, he thought, *I see all these healings, but I don't see God's kingdom coming.*

When John's disciples asked him, "Are you the Messiah?" Jesus made a definitive reply. He said:

"Go back and report to John what you have seen and heard: The blind receive sight, the lame walk, those who have leprosy are cured, the deaf hear, the dead are raised, and the good news is preached to the poor. Blessed is the man who does not fall away on account of me." [1]

If all John needed was miraculous evidence he would not have needed to send his disciples to question Jesus. John already knew about those miracles.

When John heard in prison what Christ was doing, *he sent his disciples to ask him, "Are you the one who was to come, or should we expect someone else?"* [2]

In fact, it seems that John's knowledge of the signs and wonders is actually part of the problem that raises the question, not something that is going to help fix the problem.

[1] Luke 7:20-23   [2] Matthew 11:2-3

The following imaginative conversation between John and Jesus helps clarify the issue:

JOHN: *Are you the One who was to come? Are you the Christ? Because all I see are these miracles.*

JESUS: *Exactly.*

JOHN: *No, Jesus. I mean are you the Christ? The one who will establish the kingdom of God? That's what I expected, but all I see are these miracles of healing and delivering people.*

JESUS: *Exactly.*

JOHN: *No, Jesus, you don't understand. I am in prison. This shouldn't be happening. If you really are the Messiah, you'd be setting up your kingdom authority and driving out the evil powers that are ruling over us.*

JESUS: *Exactly.*

JOHN: *Wait a minute. What do you mean by exactly? I'm looking at the things you are doing, and this doesn't look to me like what we thought it would mean to bring the kingdom of God. As nice as your ministry is, I need proof that you are the Christ who will eventually establish the kingdom.*

JESUS: ***Eventually** establish the kingdom? **Eventually**? Look at all these miracles. This is the kingdom!*

The problem with our theology today is that we have relegated the signs and wonders to a position of **evidence** of the kingdom rather than the **essence** of the kingdom. They are what God does when God comes on the scene. They are what God does when God takes charge—when we let Him rule.

"Are you the Christ?" John asks, "Because you're not doing what the coming Christ is supposed to do."

And Jesus replies, "Wrong. Look at what I am doing. That's exactly what the Christ does."

The kingdom is healing*, deliverance, and various life-giving signs and wonders. If we are not seeking that, then we are not seeking the kingdom.

If we are to be a kingdom teaching church then we must expect and make place in our theology and practice for the supernatural ministries of the kingdom.

* See Appendix B: Healing Today?

Clarify its Dimensions

What's your cosmology? That's probably not a question you've been asked before. But believe it or not, you've got an answer. That's because you have an opinion about what makes up reality—the *cosmos*. (Cosmology is the study of what makes up the universe.)

Some people believe only what they can experience with their five senses exists. That's why they don't believe in God.

Other people are willing to accept the existence of God. Maybe even other nonphysical beings such as angels.

If we are going to teach the kingdom of God, we have to sync up with the Bible's cosmology. And here's where we get stretched. Because—are you ready?—the Bible clearly expects us to believe in the existence of a satanic realm and demons, as well as a heavenly realm and angels.

The Bible expects us to go one step farther. It tells us that both the angelic realm and the demonic realm are interactive with human affairs.

And another thing... the kingdom of God has much to do with warfare on earth between heavenly hosts and demonic hoards who currently influence much of what goes on here, even though they are a defeated foe of God. If this sounds a little too strange, just keep in mind Jesus' teaching and miracles that time and time again acknowledged and attacked demonic beings. In fact, the apostle John put it bluntly that the reason the Son of God came to earth was to destroy the devil's works.[1]

While many people in our modern era would have us pass off "devil talk" as archaic and prescientific superstition, that cosmology continued to prevail at the origin of Protestantism as seen in the words penned by Martin Luther in his most famous hymn:

And though this world with devil's filled
Should threaten to undo us;
We will not fear for God hath willed
His truth to triumph through us.
The prince of darkness grim,
We tremble not for him...[2]

Any passion for God's kingdom must include an awareness and readiness to face a supernatural foe.

In fact, the apostle Paul located our only real battle for faith, righteousness and truth squarely in the realm of warfare against evil "principalities and powers" rather than flesh and blood enemies.[3]

If we want to have maximum impact that

---

[1] 1 John 3:8   [2] *A Mighty Fortress Is Our God*   [3] Ephesians 6:10-12

Our Method: Kingdom Teaching

brings rescue and restoration to multitudes of people, we must broaden the dimensions of the kingdom to encompass spiritual beings. We will have little effectiveness in community transformation until we learn to enforce kingdom authority over a destructive, hateful enemy.

Finally, the supernatural dimension doesn't just stop with spiritual warfare against demonic powers. It also involves some wonderful possibilities for communicating and partnering with God. Because the biblical cosmology includes supernatural beings, like God Himself, it also includes supernatural communication, including dreams and visions.[4]

You get the picture? To teach the kingdom requires that we also expand our minds to include possibilities for interaction with God and His angelic servants.

Yes, things can get freaky when you go there, because people can let pride and screwball ideas mess things up. But that doesn't mean these dimensions are not real, or that we should avoid them out of prejudice and fear. Far too often churches have simply closed the door to these dimensions. (See a further discussion of this problem in *Appendix C: Behind the Closed Door*.)

As a kingdom teaching church we must open the door fully and also guide wisely.

[4] Acts 8:26, 10:3, 10:10-11, 16:9

Let's take a moment to see where we are. So far we've covered:

OUR PASSION:
God's Kingdom

OUR VISION:
Maximum Impact

OUR METHOD:
Kingdom Teaching

Seek its coming.

Define its nature.

▶ **Clarify its dimensions.**

Overcome its foes.

Practice its ways.

Overcome its Foes

The kingdom of God has several foes that must be overcome in order for the kingdom of God to fully establish its presence and power here. Based on our discussion in the previous section, it comes as no surprise that **Satan is our arch enemy**. He is maliciously opposed to everything the kingdom of God is about.

The apostle Paul warns us about Satan's schemes and trickery as he engages in nonstop combat to thwart God's plans and block kingdom powers. So we make it a top priority to equip and train ourselves to discover and disarm him wherever he tries to infiltrate. This is often referred to as *spiritual warfare.* We'll go into more detail about how we approach spiritual warfare in the section about our emphases (see page 38).

However, not all kingdom foes are demonic in nature. **Sometimes we can be own worst enemy.** Things going on inside us may either stifle or flatly oppose the kingdom of God. One opponent is of particular concern here. Prejudice.

Prejudice is often identified with racial matters. And rightly so. But it can also pop up elsewhere. For example, there is such a thing as **theological prejudice**.

Racial prejudice says things like: *poor people are lazy*; or, *Jewish people are money hungry*; or *Italians are hot-headed*. Similarly, theological prejudice says things like: *all Pentecostals are anti-intellectual*; or, *all charismatics only care about spiritual experiences*.

Sometimes theological prejudice is not directed toward particular people but toward particular doctrines. For example, certain gifts of the Spirit, like speaking in tongues, are often singled out and prohibited in many churches. "If you let *them* in," it is argued with strangely similar rationales as those used in times of racial segregation, "they will only cause discord and disruption."

Other churches are not quite so opposed but still worry about potential problems. So they make them ride on the back of the bus, so to speak.

Theological prejudice also often shows itself over issues

OVERCOME ITS FOES (cont.)

of divine healing. Many people have had bad experiences associated with praying for healing. Typically this is what happens. We pray fervently for someone to be healed, like a loved one or a close friend—someone we care about deeply—and that person is not healed, maybe even dies.

In the aftermath, we may struggle with the unwanted outcome along with bitterness toward God and those fellow believers who come across as if the lack of healing was due to a lack of faith.*

This makes us angry and leaves us confused. If this happens too often or the hurt goes too deep, eventually we make gradual and subtle changes in our personal theology and, for all practical purposes, literally stop believing in healing. (Although, we may still offer token prayers, not really expecting God to heal, because we don't want our disbelief discovered.)

Eventually we gather enough biblical evidence from biblical teachers who disbelieve in healing to support our adopted viewpoint that the miraculous *signs and wonders* so prevalent in the New Testament are no longer happening today. And there it is! There's the prejudice now fully formed and functioning. It controls whose books we read and whose input we receive.

This is so unfortunate, because if it is true that the kingdom of God is, as we have seen, a matter of healing and deliverance, of supernatural ministry and communication, then the prejudicial rejection of the more "supernatural" spiritual gifts like healing, prophecy, tongues and words of knowledge, etc. actually prevent the rescuing and restoring work of God's kingdom.

As a kingdom teaching church, we recognize that our task is to make a strong case for a theology of signs and wonders today. These things are not easy to believe, whether or not we've had bad experiences. Our natural tendency to believe only what we can see and to explain all human experience and problems in scientific terms already slants us strongly away from an openness to signs and wonders.

Therefore, in order to seek God's kingdom and have maximum impact **we are committed to providing continual teaching, practice and testimony that counteracts all prejudice against the supernatural dimensions of the kingdom.**

---

* For helpful insights into why some people may not be healed see the "Five Guardrails" section in Appendix B.

Practice its Ways

Perhaps right about now you're thinking, *Yikes! All this supernatural talk is kind of out there!* You're hearing the *Twilight Zone* music in the background. That's understandable. This lofty theological talk tends to put our heads in the clouds—which is where things stay if we don't get serious about putting theory into practice.

So we believe kingdom teaching, just like piano teaching, means we insist on, "Practice. Practice. Practice." Just as piano students rehearse scales and arpeggios until their fingers are trained and skills are mastered, even so people who want to follow Jesus Christ must practice the ways of the kingdom.

In order to provide people with opportunities to practice, we toss them the keys and put them in the driver's seat even before they *feel* ready. What does that look like?

For example, if the kingdom is about rescue and restoration, we urge people to take on hard cases rather than run from them or pass them off to trained counselors. The Bible says that the counsel of Christ can be transmitted through us as His Word dwells in us richly[1] and His Spirit makes it come alive for a particular situation. But people never experience that until they find themselves in situations where they don't know what to say or how to say it.[2]

This is a basic strategy we employ as a general rule of the kingdom. It is how you practice the ways of the kingdom. Put yourself in situations that require divine help and you'll discover supernatural giftings and graces that reveal the kingdom, strengthen your faith and increase your competence.

That's how you practice. That's how we approach teaching the kingdom. In other words, start rescuing people and you'll quickly start receiving knowledge. Knowledge that comes from hands-on experience, not books.

Of course, we're not going to put anyone in the driver's seat without some basic rules of the road for faith and action. The next major section surveys our important emphases.

[1] Colossians 3:16   [2] Matthew 10:18-20

OUR Emphases: TRuth. FreeDOM. TransFORMation.

Everything we hope to be and do as a church falls under these three words: truth, freedom and transformation. They are linked together almost as tightly as the Holy Trinity. The Father, Son and Holy Spirit are distinct, yet inseparably One. So are truth, freedom and transformation.

The truth sets you free. You are transformed by the renewing of your mind. We are sanctified (i.e. morally transformed) by the truth. No one becomes actually righteous until he is no longer a slave to sin. All three work side by side, hand in hand, simultaneously. To be free is to be transformed. To be transformed is to be in your right mind. It's almost as if these three elements represent the main role of each person of the trinity. The Father represents the mind and purposes of God (truth). The Son came as our redeemer (freedom). The Spirit imparts God's holiness inwardly (transformation).

If all this is true, then it is absolutely crucial that we emphasize all three. Some churches are all about truth. But you never hear about freedom. Other churches tout freedom but are loosey-goosey about truth.

However, just as the Bible urges us to exalt Jesus at the center of everything, and the whole Trinity will ultimately be honored, even so when freedom is placed at the center of our concern, truth and transformation will find their prominence. Just as a passion for Jesus results in a passion for the Father, even so a passion for freedom results in a hunger for truth. And just as a passion for Jesus prompts the release of the Spirit, even so a passion for freedom prompts the release of transformational power.

Therefore, as a strategic priority the strongest emphasis should ultimately be placed on freedom which drives us toward truth and releases transformation. In fact, to fail to provide freedom to people while at the same time expecting them to become more Christlike is unrealistic. All people have issues that bind them up—fears, habits, thought patterns, grudges, addictions, hurts, maybe even demonic strongholds and generational sins—which make obedience to God and walking in faith much harder, if not nearly impossible. No matter how hard they try, unless people are freed from these kinds of problems they will keep falling into sin and disobedience, or doubt and failure. Transformation gets stifled.

We put it this way: **people have to get freed before they can get fixed.**

In order for freedom to be provided, however, there are several principles that must be understood and practiced.

The following pages capsulize ten principles that must be observed for freedom to occur in and through anyone's life.

#1 The Performative Nature of God's Word

In the famous story of Jesus healing the royal official's terminally sick son[1] from eighteen miles away without actually going and touching the boy, we learn a powerful lesson about how God works. He causes things to happen by the power of the spoken word. In fact, this is how God usually gets things done. He speaks **performative words.**

The creation story in Genesis starts right off with this fundamental fact. He spoke everything into existence out of nothing, starting with light. *"Let there be light," and there was light.*[2]

That's how the royal official came to believe in Jesus as God's Son, when he discovered that his son got better at the "exact time" Jesus spoke out, "Your son will live."[3] He was convinced because, *that's how the true God acts!*

All of scripture repeatedly emphasizes this principle telling us that all things are sustained by God's word[4]; faith comes by hearing God's word[5]; people are born again[6], washed[7] and sanctified[8] by the word of God; every word God speaks always accomplishes His purposes[9]; and so much more!

Therefore, this should be our number one emphasis. With simple childlike faith we should live by every word the proceeds out of the mouth of God.[10] Everything we want to be occurs as His words abide in us.[11] And everything we want to do will occur only as we hear, believe and—most importantly—speak God's words in faith, whether direct from the holy scriptures or the Holy Spirit.

The bottom line? God's word isn't just *informative*, giving us proverbs for a good life; His word is *performative*, giving us power to effect change. That's the Father's business and the tricks of the trade Jesus came to teach us.[12]

[1] John 4:46ff [2] Genesis 1:3 [3] John 4:53 [4] Hebrews 1:3 [5] Romans 10:17 [6] 1 Peter 1:23 [7] Ephesians 5:26
[8] John 17:17 [9] Isaiah 55:11 [10] Deuteronomy 8:3 [11] John 15:7 [12] John 15:15

Clearly Jesus made prayer His priority in relating to His heavenly Father and doing His earthly work—even if it meant getting up very early.[1] That fact alone should be all the evidence anybody needs that prayer must be made central to everything we do. But there's more. His curious disciples watched Jesus closely, but never asked, "Teach us to heal," or "Teach us to preach." Their only request was, "Teach us to pray."[2]

He taught them that given the choice between busy service and devoted listening, listening to Him is the one necessary thing.[3] He taught them to pray and not give up.[4] His most outlandish promises were wrapped up in the invitation to pray. *Ask and you will receive.*[5] Four times in His final hours with His disciples He repeated essentially the same promise: *I tell you the truth, my Father will give you whatever you ask in my name.*[6] Get the idea? He wants us to pray.

But in those final hours and tucked in those four promises there is a vital lesson on prayer that connects with Emphasis #1 on the Performative Word. Jesus prefaced His promise with a proviso. ***If you remain in me and my words remain in you**, ask whatever you wish, and it will be given you.*[7]

Prayer is the technology of the kingdom. It moves things, changes things and causes things to happen. But it only works if we are praying God's words. We should never try to *name it and claim it*—if what we "name" is based on our thoughts and desires. But if we have God's word on the matter, well then, by all means claim what God names.

That's how we understand "praying in the Spirit."[8] It's not necessarily about having a spiritual language. It's about being prompted and guided by the Spirit of God to pray in a certain way with certain words. It's PUI—Praying Under the Influence.

There is nothing more important than making time privately and coming together corporately to pray under the influence of the Holy Spirit. Praying God's words changes everything.

The Priority of Prayer in the Spirit #2

[1] Mark 1:35   [2] Luke 11:1   [3] Luke 10:42   [4] Luke 18:1
[5] Luke 11:9-10; Matthew 21:22; John 16:24   [6] John 16:23, 15:16   [7] John 15:7   [8] Ephesians 6:18

As we have seen, God's Word has performative power. But here's a major principle. It's power is not primarily conceptual. It's operational. It's not merely the power of an idea rolling around in the mind. God did not think, "Let there be light." He announced it even though no one was around to hear it but Himself.

The performative power of God's word lies in the delivery of His word. Only when God's word **goes out**[1] from His mouth can God's purposes on earth be accomplished.

What is true for God must also be true for His children and partners. His words must go out from our mouths. Jesus, who is our Example, the One whom we follow religiously to do the things He did, functioned according to this principle.

His ministry was all about freeing prisoners, restoring sight to the blind, releasing the oppressed. But in His inaugural address when He announced His life purpose[2], He spoke of only one action He would perform. Proclamation. He did not say He would **free** captives or **heal** the blind. He said He would **preach** freedom and recovery of sight. Every good thing He accomplished was somehow dependent on and triggered by the activity of proclamation: speaking the Father's will, speaking the Father's promises, speaking the Father's words out loud.

Our job is no less verbal. We should not just pray inside our mind. We should pray out loud when possible. We should agree vocally when scripture is publicly read and taught. It's not just the preacher who proclaims. The whole Body proclaims through uttering firm *Amens* of faith as the Word is declared. We should take every opportunity to bring a testimony (a spoken witness to God's reality and greatness) in public gatherings or private conversation which can break the power of Enemy influence[3] in people's lives and even in entrenched societal evils.

Don't wait to shout from rooftops until you're *elated*. Do so because you're *related* to the God who calls things into existence.[4]

The Importance of Proclamation

[1] Isaiah 55:11   [2] Luke 4:18-21   [3] Revelation 12:10-11   [4] Romans 4:17

34 Our Emphases: Truth. Freedom. Transformation.

Persuasive Demonstrations of the Holy Spirit

Hopefully by now it's apparent that we believe in using our minds. Whether you agree with what we think and consider important, at least we've got some clear reasons and decent logic behind our convictions. So let's be clear about this, the mind is important. The intellect is a gift from God. Using it well is our gift to Him.

Nevertheless, God's people often rely too much on what their minds can conceive and understand, either due to intellectual pride or a need to find security in what makes sense. That becomes our habit when presenting Jesus Christ to the world. We try to "reason" people into the kingdom. We try to educate them into personal freedom and wholeness.

In contrast, after years of hard experience trying to persuade people to believe and be saved, the apostle Paul settled on one strategy: ***don't rely on fine sounding arguments and persuasive words, but on demonstrations of the Spirit's power.***[1] He didn't want people to believe based on human wisdom, but on God's power.

Following his lead, we should settle for nothing short of visible evidence of God's power at work among us. We should never hide behind ambiguous rationalizations in the absence of undeniable manifestations of the Spirit of God. For example, as people often say when questioning the necessity of supernatural signs and wonders, "The greatest miracle is the miracle of salvation." But clearly that's not what Paul was referring to—this apostle who saw healings, deliverances, resurrections, prophecies, miraculous escapes from prison, etc.—when he used the phrase "demonstrations of the Spirit's power."

We must make time and space for God to do supernatural works by His power and beyond our understanding. We must not shy away from asking God to "show" Himself among us. We must offer Him opportunities when we gather together in corporate worship and prayer, in large and small group gatherings. And when those "demonstrations" are not occurring we must honestly ask ourselves, "Why not?" and seek Him fervently until they are.

---

[1] 1 Corinthians 2:4-5

#5 The Full Scope of Salvation

One of the greatest ironies in all Christian history is that the evangelical movement—the movement which can be credited with spreading the good news around the world—actually shrank the good news in the process! In its zeal to make believers, the gospel message got reduced to "get saved from your sins and go to heaven." The world asked, "How can this be?" And the church answered, "Because Jesus paid the penalty for your sins and died on the cross in your place."

That message is true, of course. The problem is it's also too tiny. It's not the whole story of the cross. It's just one salvation paradigm—one way of looking at what the cross of Christ means. This rendition of the gospel is often called the *judicial paradigm* in which salvation is viewed through the metaphor of a courtroom, including a judge, a defendant, and a guilty sentence.

However, there are other paradigms—dare we even say, more powerful and for centuries more prevalent paradigms. For example, the *Christus Victor paradigm* prevailed during the first millenium of the church and portrayed the cross of Christ as primarily a place of battle and victory over Satan to reclaim the world and its inhabitants from his dominion. That's why Handel's famous Hallelujah Chorus concludes with the resounding affirmation: *The kingdom of this world has become the kingdom of the Lord and of His Christ; and He shall reign forever and ever.*

We believe our responsibility is to teach the full scope of salvation by exposing our congregation to many biblical ways of understanding salvation. After all, if salvation comes by faith, and faith comes by hearing, then how saved you get depends on how much salvation you hear about. Yes, Jesus died on the cross to pay for our sins. But there was a lot more going on there than just making payment to get us into heaven.

So *how saved can you get?* That's been a debated question throughout the centuries. Most Christians today are taught and blindly accept a rather pessimistic view of salvation. They think, *I'm forgiven, but I'm always going to be nothing more than a sinner.* They assume that they will never really enjoy much freedom from sinful habits until they die and go to heaven. They think that the apostle Paul's hypothetical situation described in Romans is an accurate account of the way the Christian life is bound to be experienced:

> *I do not understand what I do. ... I know that nothing good lives in me. ... For I have the desire to do what is good, but I cannot carry it out. For what I do is not the good I want to do; no, the evil I do not want to do—this I keep on doing.*[1]

But is this description simply "the way it is?" Must we resign ourselves to this life of struggle and habitual moral failure? No.

The full gospel presents a much more optimistic viewpoint. The power of sin in a person's heart can be uprooted. And the damage from sin can be healed. The power is uprooted **in a moment**—in a crisis of surrender to God's complete control—through the simple exercise of faith in God's promise to fill you entirely with His Holy Spirit. The damage is healed over the course of time **in a process** as a person learns to walk in truth and live in the reality of his new self.[2] Since we are *broken people being healed* we can still sin even though we are set free from its power, because sin often arises out of personal weakness, rather than inward evil. Just think of how you snap at people you love when you've got a headache.

So we teach people how to confess the truth and "consider yourself dead to sin,"[3] then walk in truth as they learn to "put off the old man... and put on the new man."[4] But this process doesn't work until you take advantage of God's crisis work of total infilling. So we offer this infilling through proclamation and the biblical practice of impartation through "laying on hands."[5]

> See Appendix A for a complete look at this question:
> ***How Saved Can You Get?***

Entire Sanctification as Crisis and Process

[1] Romans 7:15-19   [2] Romans 6:5-8   [3] Romans 6:11   [4] Ephesians 4:22-24   [5] Acts 8:14-17; 19:6

As we've learned, God's Kingdom comes to rescue and restore broken people. Imagine yourself as God's enemy. If you're Satan, and for some vexing reason you couldn't keep a person from being rescued, what's plan B? Keep him from being restored. Keep him from discovering this full salvation we've been talking about. At least then he won't enjoy his salvation and might actually keep others from being rescued by being joyless, powerless and preoccupied with personal struggles.

Sounds like a good strategy... if you're Satan. In fact, that is Satan's strategy. All he wants you to do is **miss out** on what's possible and available. He'll do whatever it takes. He'll steal seeds of God's Word before they take root and sprout into faith.[1] He'll distract and deceive.[2] He'll keep you stewing about some past hurt. All he has to do is get you off track. He'll even mess with your body or your circumstances if he has some point of access, just to trouble your life.[3]

That's why we take seriously our authority to detect Satan's schemes and arrest Satan's power. We don't make a guessing game of it—wondering if demons are behind every human problem. We simply assume that every human problem—whether initiated by the enemy or not—can be intensified by the enemy. Or he can interfere with important help.[4] Whatever the case, it is our practice to come against him at every turn through simple prayers of resistance.[5] No big showdown. No scary close encounters. Just prayer and truth to counter his plans and lies.

It is the failure to enforce kingdom authority, renounce Satan's lies, and remove demonic interference that leaves most Christians in a place of spiritual defeat or discouragement. So we must teach people how to stand against the enemy, and provide counsel that shows people specific steps to freedom in Christ.

#7 Spiritual Warfare and Steps to Freedom

[1] Matthew 13:19   [2] Matthew 4:1-10   [3] Matthew 17:14-18   [4] Mark 4:37-41   [5] James 4:7

Our Emphases: Truth. Freedom. Transformation.

The "Greater" *Great Commission*

Most Christians are very familiar with what is known as the Great Commission.[1] We are supposed go into the whole world and make disciples by baptizing believers and teaching them to obey everything Jesus commanded His disciples.

What commands did Jesus specifically have in mind? Love your neighbors? Turn the other cheek? Take up your cross? When the Great Commission is taught these are the kinds of commands that are assumed. Moral commands.

But is that what Jesus' disciples would have thought? Probably not. It makes more sense to assume that their minds would have connected this **final commission** from Him with their **first commission** from Him. That is, they would have heard Him saying, *Teach your disciples to obey the same commands I gave when I first made you my disciples.* What were those commands?

They are found in Matthew 10:1-8 which bears a striking resemblance to Matthew 28:18-20. In both Jesus passes on His authority. In both Jesus sends them out, saying "go!" It's almost a repeat performance. So it is likely they would have been remembering the commands He gave that first day, which were:

As you go, preach this message: "The kingdom of heaven is near." Heal the sick, raise the dead, cleanse those who have leprosy, drive out demons. Freely you have received, freely give.

These are the *first commission* commands Jesus instructed His first disciples in the *great commission* to pass on to all subsequent disciples—commands to do miracles of healing and deliverance.

Now remember, Jesus doesn't give commands which cannot be obeyed. Being a disciple requires obeying those commands. Imagine that! Supernatural ministry is still the name of the game. And you're supposed to be involved. Perhaps the great commission is greater than you thought.

[1] Matthew 28:18-20

# Situational Spiritual Gifts

By now nothing should be clearer than our belief in the necessity and availability of supernatural power and resources for salvation and ministry. No one—not you, not anybody—can be set free and transformed without God doing miraculous works of grace through His followers.

That means He has to give us the tools and skills to do the work He has commissioned us to do in the "greater commission." And He does. The apostle Paul tells us about spiritual gifts.[1] These are special abilities that the Holy Spirit provides to serve inside and outside the church.

Unfortunately, the common understanding of spiritual gifts actually limits our ability to experience and function in those gifts. Here's how most Christians are taught to think about spiritual gifts. "Every Christian has at least one God-given gift. You need to discover your gift and then use it." Many churches actually administer so-called *spiritual gift inventories* to help people find theirs.

Two problems with this approach. It confuses spiritual gifts with God-given abilities. Second, it promotes the idea of responding to some situation or need only if you feel capable.

This is not how God often works. Frequently He puts us into situations where our lack of capability requires His on-the-spot enablement. An effective Christian teacher[2] and healer used an analogy: *It's like you have an empty tool box, and God sends you on a job. You have to go to the job trusting that when you get there, you'll open your tool box and find the right tool inside.*

That's our understanding of spiritual gifts. They are different than God-given abilities you have all the time. Spiritual gifts are situational. They come and go at God's discretion. Our privilege is to be on call for any job and open to receiving any gift. That way we get amazed and God gets the credit.

[1] 1 Corinthians 12:7-11   [2] John Wimber, founder of the Vineyard churches movement

With all this emphasis on supernatural power and ministry, you might be tempted to think that we believe God snaps His fingers and turns us into superhero-type Christians. Nothing could be farther from the truth.

We believe that engaging in kingdom ministry and having maximum impact requires certain traits that only come by a commitment to being a radical person. Sold out. Kind of like bungee jumping.

We describe this spirit of radical discipleship by identifying six character traits that we promote and pursue.

Radical Generosity: *a readiness to give away what you yourself need.*

Purposeful Simplicity: *live an uncluttered life not for personal peace but for single-minded service.*

Aggressive Peace: *war against that which makes war; destroy what destroys, kill that which kills.*

Holy Desperation: *a continual motivating sense of urgency to be and do all that God makes possible.*

Selfless Courage: *personal sacrifice for some worthy purpose in the face of fear and loss.*

Expressive Love: *Take what's true and make it tangible. Help people become clear and certain about things they need to understand.*

None of the above traits occurs without what we call **spoudazo**, an anglicized version of a Greek word used over and over in the New Testament often translated "make every effort."[1] Spoudazo is when you live up to your capacity in these character traits and then trust God to supplement your efforts with His enabling power.

Six Traits of Radical Disciples #10

2 Peter 1:5,15;3:14; Romans 14:19; Luke 13:24; Ephesians 4:3; Hebrews 12:14

OUR CHaLLenge: ERADicate poverty

To live kingdom principles so fully and effectively that we see the eradication of all forms of poverty in our community* in 20 years.

At first glance this challenge hardly seems "spiritual." Especially in light of the previous pages with so much emphasis on the supernatural dimensions and activities of the kingdom of God. But keep this in mind. If we believe anything, we believe in a God who rescues and restores. Everyone. Especially the most lost and helpless. So the poor are at the center of His attention. Second, JFK's words (facing page) are so true. Huge challenges have a way of marshalling all of our best energies, skills and beliefs. No one makes great efforts who is not caught up in a great cause. Eradicating poverty requires our best material and spiritual resources, and the employment of all our natural and supernatural abilities. In 1962, few believed we would land a man on the moon by the end of that decade. That just goes to show you...

* Our challenge to eradicate poverty in our community is not our only concern about poverty relief. We are also committed to address global poverty in many ways, especially focusing on the "poorest of the poor".

42 *Our Challenge: Eradicate Poverty*

> We choose to go to the moon in this decade and do the other things, not because they are easy, but because they are hard, because that goal will serve to measure and organize the best of our energies and skills, because that challenge is one that we are willing to accept, one we are unwilling to postpone and one which we intend to win.
> - John F. Kennedy
> September 12, 1962

the eradicati

WHAT WE MEAN BY "POVERTY"

Poverty is not a thing. It is an absence of something. Just as darkness is the absence of light, **poverty is the absence of resources, opportunity and access to basic elements that are needed to prosper**. So there are varying degrees and kinds of poverty in America. Poverty is not just financial. It's a constellation of problems.

Poverty is a single mom who was not promoted at her low-wage, mega-store job, because although she got government provided dentures, she could not afford the $250 adjustment to make them wearable. Hence, her appearance prevented her promotion, which prevented her from having regular hours to be home with her mentally retarded daughter after school, forcing her to pay for after school care, which took 25% of her take home pay, which kept her from getting her car fixed when it broke down—and she had no one to help. All of which led to the loss of her job.

The kind of poverty in America is like a person just barely below the surface of the water. It takes the infusion of relatively little financial help to stop the vicious cycles and lift them up for air.

But it takes social capital—someone being there as a guide, a support and an advocate when help is needed. It is the lack of this kind of help at the right time, in the right amounts, and the right way that keeps people being pulled back down beneath the surface when they are desperately trying to stay afloat.

The constant knockdowns in turn shape and reinforce self-defeating habits and attitudes.

Our Challenge: Eradicate Poverty

What we mean by "Eradicate"

To eradicate poverty does not mean there will be no poor people—guaranteed. Both the Old Testament, as well as Jesus said that the poor will always be present. Unfortunate circumstances will occur, unwise decisions will be made, work hampering disabilities will happen that will strip people of their opportunities to prosper.

Rather, to eradicate poverty means that all people have access to meaningful chances to prosper. If people will not take advantage of those good chances, then the problem is not poverty, but pride or stubbornness or rebellion. In other words, if you put $100,000 in the bank to provide for your child's education, and he chooses not to go to college, the problem was not lack of resources but for whatever reason the lack of willingness to take advantage of the opportunity.

Thus we can say to have eradicated poverty in our community in twenty years if all people have access to meaningful opportunities to prosper, and if we have found effective ways to help people access those opportunities. That means if we are providing job training and job placement (an opportunity to prosper), but the person's problem is the lack of dentures, or child care, then the opportunity to prosper is not meaningful to them.

How we Make Plans

There is often a fundamental difference between the way the world devises a plan and the way God dictates a plan. The world devises plans by adopting a vision and then establishing a series of goals, objectives and tasks to guide decisions. The world delegates assignments, sets timetables and requires measurement to gage progress. All of this is very valuable.

But often God's plans require that we head toward an ultimate goal knowing only the first step. He does not give guarantees in the form of mind-satisfying strategies. He expects us to take action based primarily on His Word. And what's more, the first step is usually one which requires boldness. It may seem foolish. Or deadly. God says, "Do it. Start crossing the sea.[1] It will part. Just march around the walls.[2] They will fall. Just give away your lunch.[3] It will feed a multitude. Just step out from the boat.[4] You won't sink."

[1] Exodus 14:15ff [2] Joshua 6:2ff [3] Mark 6:37ff [4] Matthew 14:28ff

IS POVERTY ERADICATION "DOABLE"?

People often face a question that makes them wonder whether there's any point in moving so aggressively against poverty. *Is there any hope for getting rid of poverty?* Will all our efforts make any difference? After all, they point out, even Jesus said there will always be poor people. Even more troubling to those of us who want to end poverty, Jesus said this in response to one of His disciples who was suggesting the idea of giving thousands of dollars to the poor rather than "wasting" some valuable burial perfume on Him.

Do Jesus' words mean there is no point trying? Does that mean any attempts we make are little more than **a measly drop in the bucket?** Should we throw up our hands as if the impossibility of the task nullifies the importance of the attempt?

Lots of people quietly allow the fact of unrelenting poverty to justify the lack of strategic plans for poverty eradication.

Before that line of thinking starts making too much sense, let's change the object under consideration from poverty to physical suffering.

If Jesus had similarly observed, "There will always be sick people among you," would that be a reason to stop trying to find ways to eradicate pain and suffering? Of course not.

Just because something is rampant in epidemic proportions—whether disease or poverty—doesn't mean you stop fighting the epidemic. On the contrary, you fight all the harder.

When Jesus said that the poor would always be around, He was not meaning, "There's not much you can do about the poor, so don't worry about trying too hard." He only meant that His followers would have plenty of other opportunities to serve the poor.

But still, we want to know in advance if poverty eradication, or anything even anywhere close to it, is doable.

So consider the following four factors.

"The poor will always be with you..."
—Jesus (John 12:8)

46 Our Challenge: Eradicate Poverty

1. GOD'S PLAN. God established a system of economic laws intended to eradicate poverty among His people every 50 years. Therefore, it's doable because God is behind it. *With God all things are possible. (Matthew 19:26; Mark 9:23)*

2. BIG MONEY. Money doesn't solve poverty; but poverty won't be solved without money, major amounts of it. Even though poverty involves many factors that cluster around every needy person differently, almost all of these factors will require some expenditure of money.

3. FAITHFUL FRIENDS. Most poor people in our community can be lifted out of poverty with modest amounts of financial assistance in combination with the personal assistance of a faithful friend and advisor.

4. RAW NUMBERS. There are fewer than 1500 people in poverty in our community. If 200 people volunteer to be faithful friends to one family until their life situation improves it would take less than 15-20 years before every poor person and family had a viable opportunity to be lifted out of poverty.

Turn to the next page to see how we address each of these four factors with a four-point plan of action.

"What is so little among so many?"
  —The disciples. (John 6:9)

1 Seek SPIRIT-PROVIDED GIFTS OF Service

The very fact that poverty is more than a financial problem means that those who want to set people free from its grip must be prepared to discern and address an array of human needs. In all cases there will be a spiritual dimension that is key to providing real lasting help.

For example, in some cases the poverty is a result of chronic physical problems that prevent work and keep people in a state of indebtedness to medical providers. Sometimes—more than you may think—those chronic physical problems are the tormenting tactics of the enemy of our souls who intends to keep people in a state of confusion and defeat. There may be an "access point" that this viral enemy uses to mount his attacks which must be permanently blocked. Or, there may be some long-standing effects of a family sin—often called a "generational sin"—committed decades ago that must be nullified through spiritual warfare and a process of renunciation. In these situations the Spirit-provided gifts of discernment and faith must function effectively. Otherwise, no amount of financial aid or counseling will break the habits and circumstances of poverty.

The personal struggles people in poverty face may not be so directly demonic as the previous examples. Instead, their problems may arise due to any combination of limiting factors such as lack of education, training, advocacy, emotional intelligence, life skills, healthy habits, etc. Nevertheless, in all cases the enemy will take advantage of these deficiencies to make matters worse or obstruct proper help. We put it this way: Satan may not always *instigate* our problems, but he will always try to *intensify* or *interfere*.

He must be blocked by people who know how to handle his tactics. This supernatural assistance will give needy people the best possible chance to find help through the natural resources available.

As we have stated many times previously, our #1 strategy is to maintain our primary emphasis on prayer and train our people in functioning with the supernatural ministry gifts of the Holy Spirit. Based on feasibility factor #1 (God's Plan) on the previous page, we can count on God to provide every possible necessary tool to fulfill our challenge to eradicate poverty.

Without using these Spirit-provided gifts our efforts to liberate people from poverty—or any other debilitating problem—will be no more effective than sending a sentimental Hallmark® card.

Our Challenge: Eradicate Poverty

2 free up Big Money

There are numerous services to the needy that currently exist. Whether faith-based or not, most have something worthwhile to offer. The problem is that all of them have way too little money to meet the existing levels and types of needs they face on a daily basis. They can't hire enough staff. They don't have enough to give. What local agencies and service organizations could do with major budget increases!

On top of that, there is always a need to provide new services that currently do not exist.

In either case, they need an influx of money that just isn't there.

We have a creative plan. It sounds counterintuitive, but it works like this. Before we can fill up poverty relief services with plenty of money, we must first *free up* millions of dollars currently bound up in consumer debt. To state the plan oddly: *we attack poverty by focusing on middle class debt.*

It works like this.

A large majority of middle class families have consumer debt that traps a big chunk of their income. Christian people who want to help the poor often find their desire for generosity restricted by their debt. What if the average family could reduce their monthly indebtedness in two years by, say, $500 per month in such way that they would want to use a portion of that savings, say $100, to help the poor? And what if that plan could grow that group of new givers exponentially from 50 to 1000 in ten years?

The net result in just ten years would be annually $1.2 million! In just ten years! In 20 years that amount would more than quadruple!

Of course, that's just a drop in the bucket in relation to the national need. But not so in our community with only 1500 people in poverty.

You say, *What's the plan? Let's get started.* Good. That's just what we say.

So here's the secret to poverty eradication: identify and mobilize people who are ready to take up their cross to follow Jesus in **His way** of salvation. And His way of salvation always involves **substitutionary debt payment.**

That's a mouthful, but turn the page to get an easy, breezy theology lesson.

3. Employ Substitutionary Debt Payment

When Jesus died on the cross, a good part of what He was doing involved paying the price for our sins. As sinners, we were all living under the penalty for our sins—eternal separation from God. But Jesus paid that penalty for us. He *substituted* Himself in our place and *paid our debt*.[1]

That's where we get the official term **substitutionary debt payment.** And that's a large part of what the cross of Christ means.

So if Jesus commands all His disciples to take up their cross and follow Him, there must be some form of **substitutionary debt payment** (SDP) involved. Just like Jesus who paid for the bad consequences of other's choices, His disciples must do the same to demonstrate the meaning of the cross and the love of Jesus Christ.

One profound and relevant way to engage in the SDP work of the cross in these days of such back-breaking debt is to literally help pay a portion of someone's debt that enslaves them.

This is both the heart beat and creative plan behind the strategy to eradicate poverty. That creative plan calls for SDP to function in two ways.

First, SDP is directed toward liberating people from consumer debt. Second, it is directed toward families in poverty.

SDP for Consumer Debt. The plan calls for willing people to share enough of the debt load of another person/family for up to two years to help them break free of debt and adopt sound financial habits, which include giving to the poor. The plan involves serving as accountability partners to help recipients organize their finances, develop a debt reduction plan, and stick to a budget. As stated on the previous page, the net result of this financial liberation will mean thousands of new dollars pouring into poverty relief.

SDP for Poverty-stricken People. The biggest reason for failure in poverty relief programs is the lack of close partners who walk alongside of the needy *as long as it takes* (the key attitude) to bring about lasting change. We all know what it means to go "all out" for the welfare of a child or a family member. We believe every Christian should make room in his or her life at any given point in time for at least one extra person/family whom they will love and support like their own family. The amount of time, energy, and resources it takes to serve like that requires real sacrifice. It's a real cross. But *a real cross is what it takes to bring about real transformation*. We hope every person in our congregation when asked, "Who are you walking alongside?" will always have a current answer.

[1] Isaiah 53:6

4 facilitate A GOOD system

All these highfalutin' plans sound good on paper. But they will fall far short no matter how many folks we can inspire, if we don't have an effective system that can handle the magnitude of the numbers we have to deal with.

That's why it is important to have a coordinating ministry that can match people appropriately and guide the resourcing processes that must happen both formally and informally.

For example, imagine just one case of liberating a family from consumer debt. You have to ask: *how much credit card debt do they have? How many cards do they have? How much extra per month will it take to pay off perhaps two of those cards in two years?* They need to be matched with a family that can help with that much money. This kind of wise matching requires a well-constructed and managed system to help people succeed.

Even if people get matched appropriately, most helping people are not trained as "financial counselors" or skilled in problem-solving. Most of these helping people need some degree of guidance and customized training that shows them how to counsel the needy people they are helping. And face it, needy people often get themselves into some complicated problems that require highly trained people to know what to do.

It's like any kind of counseling. Many times fellow Christians can counsel each other effectively by tapping into the general wisdom of the word of God, applied situationally by the prompting of the Spirit and illustrated by personal experience. It's what the apostle Paul called letting the "word of Christ dwell in you richly."[2]

But then there are times when the situation calls for the specialized training of a professional counselor.

Our systems to eradicate poverty must be facilitated by a resourcing center that can bring expertise and people together, helping friends mentor, and helping those in need get the best assistance possible.

A coordinating and resourcing center that fills that bill is the **Jubilee House**. This ministry grew out of the vision to eradicate poverty based on this substitutionary debt payment philosophy. It is just one piece of evidence that God will help His people fulfill His purposes with His miracles that supplement human efforts given toward compassion and transformation.

The heart of it all... Each family. Reach one family. Every 2-3 years.

[2] Colossians 3:16

Our Hope: God's Nature

Our vision for maximum impact is based on God's nature being love and His stated will for the salvation of the whole world. We are convinced that God is honored and pleased as we set our sights on having maximum impact.

A detrimental flaw in the common American evangelical view of salvation is that Jesus' death on the cross is primarily about you and me as individuals. The average person sees salvation as person-centered, or to use a fancy but important word: anthropocentric. You can trace the influence of this view of salvation in our music. From American gospel music born in the revival period of the 1800s to many contemporary worship songs, our view of salvation is person-centered.

It's not that individuals are not precious to God. It's just that we as individuals are not the center nor the end purpose of God's salvation plan.

The only proper way to relate to God is to make Him the center of all things, not ourselves. That means somehow even our view of salvation must keep God at the center.

To help you break free of the man-centered view of salvation in favor of a much bigger view let's consider five key individuals at major moments in biblical history.

Consider Noah. To be sure he was especially blessed. He and his little family were spared from death—saved from the great flood that wiped out the world's inhabitants. But the purpose of all this individual blessing was to bring about something even greater.

Noah's individual blessing was for God's purpose of establishing a fresh irrevocable covenant with the whole world, including animals.[1]

Consider Abraham. To be sure he was especially chosen by God and individually blessed. God blessed him with a son in his old age, with years of provision and a long life. But the purpose of all this individual blessing was to bring about something even greater.

His individual blessing was for God's purpose of creating a great nation through whom the entire world would be blessed.[2]

Consider Moses. Who has ever had the privilege of communicating with God so directly, so regularly? What a remarkable individual blessing! Who has ever had the power and privilege of confronting great rulers and forcing them to give in to his demands without any powerful army to back up his threat? But the purpose of this individual blessing was to bring about something even greater.

His individual blessing was for God's purpose of bringing His people out of oppression into freedom and a place of perpetual blessing.[3]

Consider David. He was blessed with great strength resulting in astounding victories. He was elevated to the level of king. He was even called a man after God's own heart. But the purpose of all this individual blessing was to bring about something even greater.

His individual blessing was for God's purpose of establishing a permanent kingdom of the Messiah with worship—the enthronement of God—at its very heart.[4]

Consider Paul. He was blessed with a life-changing encounter with God who spoke to him

[1] Genesis 9:8-11   [2] Genesis 12:2-3   [3] Exodus 3:7-10   [4] 2 Samuel 7:8-16

audibly, who appeared to him visibly, who taught him personally, who gifted him miraculously and who saved him from persecution and death frequently. But the purpose of all this individual blessing was to bring about **something even greater.**

His individual blessing was for God's purpose of extending the invitation of the gospel of salvation to the non-Jewish world.[5]

In every case of individual blessing God had a purpose whose scope far surpassed the individual himself. No matter how much we have been blessed by God's saving grace and watchful care, we must also say: *The purpose of all this individual blessing is to bring about something even greater.*

God-centered salvation is **immeasurably vast**!

If you're really involved in God's plan of salvation, inevitably it is going to be about something big. That is what we should set our sight on.

The knowledge of God is supposed to cover the earth.[6]

God's plan of salvation sprang from His love for the **whole world**—including all creation, not just human beings.[7]

God's passion for all people in the whole world is unquenchable. Jesus taught a parable about a shepherd who had one missing sheep out of 100 and how he left the 99 safe sheep to find that lost sheep.[8] This is often used as an illustration showing God's concern for the individual. But the greater lesson is that God (the Shepherd) is passionate to have everyone in his "flock", not losing even one.

Jesus often pushed His disciples toward thinking big. He told them they could move mountains with even small amounts of faith.[9] He urged them to prove themselves to be His disciples by asking for anything in his name and bearing much fruit.[10] And if that weren't mind-blowing enough, He promised that they would do collectively greater things than He had done.[11]

On one occasion Jesus spent some private time counseling an outcast woman and leading her to life-changing salvation. Her conversion testimony was so remarkable that her whole town came out to see Jesus. As they were approaching, Jesus urged His followers to notice that the entire multitude was like a harvest of people like this woman just waiting to be brought into the kingdom of God.[12]

And finally, God's vision for the salvation of the whole world is embedded in **the ultimate commission** Jesus gave His disciples to go into all the world making disciples, starting in their own local city and then gradually moving outward regionally, nationally and globally.[13] To make that possible He sent his Spirit to create and empower the church.

God-centered salvation creates a whole people to save a whole world!

God-centered salvation validates lofty expectations! It proves that God must work powerfully in our lives. If salvation is this big and involves God's huge passion for the whole world, and if that

---

[5] Acts 9:15; 26:17-18 [6] Isaiah 11:9 [7] Romans 8:19-21 [8] Luke 15:3-7 [9] Matthew 17:20 [10] John 15:7-8 [11] John 14:12 [12] John 4:35 [13] Acts 1:8

requires a whole nation of empowered ambassadors,[14] then it stands to reason it would be required that we each and we together would be functioning at a level of **power and abilities** far above our natural abilities.

Anyone who argues that the miracles of the kingdom as displayed in the New Testament are extinct, suffers from a low view of salvation. If God is out to save the whole world, **the same supernatural manifestations** which characterized the early Christian movement and maximized their efforts are still necessary today.

It is God's intention to cover the earth… to not lose any one… and you, and I, and we together can be involved. In fact, He intends that we together can be involved in **doing great things**.

Therefore, we must set our sights on having maximum impact. God's nature and the resulting nature of His salvation is the basis of our hope and, consequently, the confirmation of our vision.

So now it's a good time to restate our definition of **maximum impact:** *As many people as possible having as much evidence as necessary to come to faith and wholeness in Jesus Christ.*

Setting our sights on maximum impact means we must move from thinking about one more soul at a time to one million souls. We must ask ourselves this question: *What would we do differently if we refused to be content with minimal impact and insisted that our efforts as a church must make maximum impact in the face of such massive need?*

We would not be content to simply hold the sick with Mother Teresa-like compassion, if it is also possible in many cases to heal the sick with Jesus-like competence.

We would look at time differently. We would look at money differently. We would look at our families differently.

We would have to experience the things of the kingdom in our immediate lives in order to have the confidence necessary to go global.

Paradoxically, such a global view of salvation, the immensity of world need and the principle of maximum impact means we have to be more serious about ourselves than most Christians are brave enough to be. Are we kingdom-first people? Do our collective lives present **credible evidence** of an all-loving, all-powerful God? Do we know how to function effectively in the power of God's Spirit? Do we know how to seek God? Are we willing to wait for God? Do we really believe?

This is why we must focus our attention on developing mature disciples of Jesus Christ. So it's time to take a look at our discipleship goal.

---

[14] 2 Corinthians 5:19-20

OUR DISCIPLESHIP GOAL:
experience. extend.

To produce fully-devoted followers of Jesus Christ who embrace truth, enter freedom, and *experience* transformation and then *extend* truth, freedom and transformation to a needy world.

As you read our discipleship goal, right away you'll notice that it's a two-parter. It's about what the individual becomes, so that each individual brings his or her experience of transformation into the world.

Deep down many Christians are paralyzed by the feeling that they have little to offer people in their world. They see the confusion, brokenness, doubts and dysfunction in the lives of their neighbors and co-workers. And they fundamentally question whether anything they say can make a dent, much less provide solutions. So they keep silent.

That's where our discipleship goal begins. We aren't trying to make "good Christians" who behave well and vote right. As a kingdom-teaching church we try to create learning environments in which our people experience profound and permanent encounters with God who obliterates their confusion, brokenness, doubt and dysfunction. Then they can go into the world with enthusiastic assurance, "This is what God did for me. I know He can do it for you."

Our learning environment emphasizes truth as discovered in God's Word and His world interpreted though reason, tradition and experience. But keep this in mind: scripture is always in first place—*prima scriptura*—as the place we expect to encounter God speaking performative words that transform. Reason, tradition and experience are vital as aids to hearing the unabridged, unobstructed words of God. But only God's words transform.

Our learning environment emphasizes freedom through ministries like "Steps to Freedom" and a fundamental conviction that no one is doomed to live with any addiction, dysfunctional habit, chronic sin or personal flaw that impedes progress in spiritual growth and obedience.

Our learning environment emphasizes transformation through the application of God's word and involvement in others-oriented service, combined with loving accountability.

A word about CHILDREN'S MINISTRY. All of the things we believe about truth, freedom and transformation apply to kids as well. The main difference is that children are typically less dysfunctional and broken. So our ministry to them is designed to teach God's Word and a pattern of living that can prevent future problems and ground them in faith and kingdom truths and practices.

That means we emphasize prayer, faith, missions, service, and small group interaction much like our adult discipleship ministries.

Children are disciples too!—often times much more ready to believe and obey than adults.

TURN THE PAGE TO DISCOVER HOW WE SET UP OUR LEARNING ENVIRONMENT IN THREE VENUES.

OUR VENUES: PURPOSEFUL FOCUS.

Be honest. Don't you sometimes feel like everything is out of control? What's the antidote? Simplify? Focus? Good. We all know what to do. The problem is doing it. It's like cleaning out the garage so you can start using it for the car again. You have to start throwing things out. *But not my sports trophies from Junior High! And this old microwave—it still works. No, not my collection of old National Geographics!* Sorry, but if you're ever going to use the garage for what it was intended, you're going to have part with a lot of stuff. You're going to have to hack away at those sentimental attachments. You're going to have to send that box of old grandfather clock parts you've had for twenty years to the Great Yard Sale in the Sky!

The same is true when it comes to simplifying anything, even churches. Some stuff has to be chucked. People argue, "It still works." Maybe so. But things that are still *usable* may not be *useful*. They gotta go.

Churches have simply got to stop trying to be a Walmart offering shelves stocked with something for everyone in just the right size and color. We must simplify. Focus. It's healthier. And in the long run we'll actually get more done, because we'll have room to do what we're called to do. The following pages tell how we focus our efforts and programming around three simple venues for ministry and what they are designed to accomplish.

VENUE	PURPOSE	MODE
 **LARGE GROUP GATHERINGS**	**evangelize seekers** — To evangelize is to bring good news to people who are seeking for something they need. Consequently, we see no strong distinction between Christian believers and those who are not yet believers. We all are still seeking. So large group gatherings are the perfect place to point people to what they need to discover—whether it's finding Jesus, or finding spiritual gifts for service.	**proclamation** — The proclamation of truth releases the creative power of truth that opens the eyes of the heart and creates or rekindles faith. Truth is proclaimed in preaching, but also in demonstrative acts of worship and affirmation.
 **MID-SIZE CLASSES**	**edify believers** — To edify is to build people up in their faith. This requires both impartation and integration of biblical knowledge. People need to know what is true and why. That's *impartation*. They also need biblical knowledge and principles that fit together into a coherent worldview. That's *integration*. We provide systematic instruction that shapes sound minds and sure faith.	**instruction** — Instruction supplies clear insights, solid answers and memorable learning from gifted teachers who have faced the right questions, studied the relevant resources and arrived at sound conclusions.
 **SMALL GROUPS**	**equip followers** — To equip is to provide people with tools, skills and practice that result in confidence and effectiveness. People are hesitant to follow Jesus into areas of ministry if they don't feel somewhat prepared and supported. We follow the small group model Jesus employed to do that equipping. *Care. Share. Prayer. Dare.*—Four rhyming words about our small groups that say it all!	**application** — Jesus warned against gaining knowledge without taking action. *Be doers, not hearers only.* Application is the vital step that translates learning into life patterns. It is best attempted with close friends who hold each other accountable.

DESIRED RESULT	MOVEMENT DIRECTION
hearts Opened *with vision, hope and response* People have to be able to see what's possible. That's *vision*. Who can we become? What can we accomplish individually and collectively? But most people are skeptical about "possibility" pep talks, unless they have a firm basis for believing the vision. That's *hope*. It's not a fingers-crossed leap of unreasonable faith. We base our vision of unbridled possibilities on the unfailing character and promises of God, and show people how to make a vigorous, practical *response*.	**seeker to believer** Everyone starts out as a seeker—a person looking for answers, trying to understand what's true and hopefully wanting to line up with reality. Eventually they will wind up "believing" something in relation to what they are looking for. They may be an agnostic wondering if God is real. They may be a Christian wondering if prayer is real. Our goal in the large group gatherings is to help people, no matter what they are seeking, to find the truth about what's real and what's possible, and settle their questions. In short we want them to know—to really believe—the truth that will set them free.
minds Shaped *by faith, knowledge and commitment* Since we are transformed by the renewing of our mind, the mind must be carefully shaped. First by *faith*, then by *knowledge*. The other way around produces people who believe only what their mind already comprehends and confirms. Transformation won't occur that way. So, the first priority of instruction is to intelligently support the claims and ways of God's kingdom no matter how hard to imagine, then call for a hearty *commitment* to those claims.	**believer to follower** Once people enter into a relationship with God as a believer in Jesus Christ, an unfortunate but common thing often happens. They become a person whose faith is expressed primarily through adhering to a set of beliefs. In short, they remain merely a believer. Jesus never wanted faith to end there—just believing the Bible or the Apostles Creed. Instead, He called people to faith in Him so that they would follow Him. Our goal in our mid-size classes is to provide knowledge and proof of our amazing belief system so convincingly that people drop everything else and follow Jesus, just like the first disciples.
wills trained *with love, skills and tasks* People have good intentions but rarely accomplish all that's possible. Why? The will to act must be trained with the right ways to act. Or else failing attempts to follow Jesus take all the air out of our good intentions. First, the will must learn to act with love or actions amount to nothing. Then the will must be guided with skills so that actions move along proven paths. Finally, no one learns without doing. Hands-on tasks give the necessary practice.	**follower to transformer** Sometimes people volunteer enthusiastically for something before they know what they are getting themselves into. That's one big reason why we have wedding ceremonies that spell out the nature of marriage very clearly. Unfortunately many Christians do not fully appreciate the fact that Jesus calls His followers to continue His work of world transformation. Therefore, we want to make sure people understand what they "signed on" for and help them ask every question and gain every skill necessary to be a powerful transformer.

OUR PROVISION: RESTORATIVE WORK

Those who join Jesus in Kingdom work find rest and reward.

As you've read this book you've probably noticed that it is very much about activism. A call to some kind of action appears on nearly every page. Over and over the topics focus on doing, serving, giving and sacrificing. The challenges and standards are set very high. To say yes requires boldness and energy. You might have even found yourself getting out of breath just reading along.

In that regard the tone and spirit of this book are somewhat counter-cultural. Our culture worries about burnout. Cultural voices urge us to set boundaries to protect ourselves. Our culture urges the average Christian to be careful about doing, doing, doing. It points to the dangers of a "performance" mentality that leaves people laboring under the fear of never doing enough. You'll even hear Christian teachers and counselors telling us to prioritize *being* over *doing*. "Who you are is more important than what you do" is the conventional wisdom.

Of course, we understand those concerns. So we conclude this book by suggesting five guiding principles for finding spiritual rest and personal restoration in the midst of the challenges of following Jesus.

1. Don't try to *separate* being *from* doing.

People who stress *who you are is more important than what you do* don't want you to feel like your worth is based on how much you accomplish or how well you do. This is a valid concern. Many people think they have to gain acceptance from God or others through hard work. But does that mean we should set "being" above "doing" as a priority? Does that even make sense?

Think about it. God is love. That's His being. But love is action. In other words, God does what He is and is what He does. That's the way things work. We should not pretend they can be separated. Because of who you are, you do what you do. And because of what you do, you are who you are.

Don't devalue the importance of performing (doing). The real safeguard against burnout is to do only what God wants you to do. That's when you'll discover the following paradox…

2. *True rest is found paradoxically in the process of co-laboring with Christ.*

One day Jesus issued an invitation to anyone and everyone who was "weary and heavy laden" to come to Him, and He would give them rest.[1] But here's the odd thing. He didn't offer them some kind of spiritual couch on which to relax. In fact, He didn't offer a respite from work at all. Rather, He invited them into a different way of working.

Using the familiar image of His day of two oxen pulling a plow, He invited people to voluntarily step under His yoke and work beside Him. To His agricultural-savvy listeners this metaphor clearly implied that He would take the lead, and His yokefellows would draw from His expertise ("learn of me") and strength. In so doing— in the very process of laboring— they would find rest for their souls.

Turns out, the cure for weariness or burnout isn't R&R. It's RW. *Restorative work.* It isn't setting boundaries, or taking a little time

[1] Matthew 11:28-30

"**just for me**." It isn't looking for balance. Though all these things are important. It's looking to Jesus—moving when He moves, stopping when He stops—and discovering how you can draw from His divine power[2] to accomplish His divine purposes. Can anything be more invigorating?

Does this mean you'll never be able to stop or slow down and relax? Of course not. But how and when that relaxation will come has to do with the next principle...

3. *Resist the temptation to be your own shepherd.*

In the most famous of all biblical Psalms, we are told that the Lord is our Shepherd. *He* makes us lie down in green pastures; *He* leads us beside still waters; *He* restores our soul.[3]

From the very beginning of human history with Adam and Eve, the chief temptation of humankind is to take matters into our own hands to obtain what we need.[4] So it's no wonder that in this matter of obtaining rest and restoration, we are strongly tempted to be our own shepherd. We will figure out how, when and where to find green pastures for spiritual nourishment, still waters for spiritual refreshment, and rest for our souls.

No matter how convincing or compelling the advice, it is not our domain to make these decisions. We need boundaries. Yes. But we do not set them. He does. We need times for personal space, but we do not schedule them at our discretion. And yes, we need breathers—green pastures and still waters. We can't handle non-stop service. But the Lord is our Shepherd not we ourselves. He knows when. He knows what and how much. When we try to work out self-care in our own wisdom to guarantee our own rest and restoration, we will inevitably fall into the category of those who are trying to "save themselves." This always backfires.[5]

4. *Seeking God's permission yields a sense of balance and peace.*

If the Lord is our shepherd, then obviously it is of paramount importance that we learn to listen for and recognize His voice. Jesus said that is exactly what His sheep will do.[6]

All of this places upon us the need to be in close communication with our heavenly Father. As we become more and more adept at recognizing His voice and following His instructions, we not only enjoy the blessings of His perfect counsel, but

[2] Peter 1:3   [3] Psalm 23:1-3   [4] Genesis 3:1-6   [5] Luke 9:24   [6] John 10:3-4

we have a calm sense of balance and peace even when we are hard at work.

The secret to hearing His voice, beside immersing ourselves is God's Word, is to live a permission-seeking life. Here's why.

Our *culture of opportunity* conditions us to believe that if something is not wrong it's automatically OK to pursue it. We think anything morally acceptable comes packaged with built-in permission. This is not true.

Even in our Christian culture, we are led to believe that having a passion for something good and the personal gifts and strengths to accomplish it, implies that God has designed us and unleashed us to pursue it. In fact, we are told this is how you know God's will.

Again, this is not necessarily true.

Something can be good, you can be gifted and even feel called, but you still have to seek God's permission before you act.

In other words, never assume you have God's permission until you explicitly seek it. When this becomes your habit, your listening skills will become highly sensitized and you will find it much easier the receive the Lord's shepherding instructions. You'll know when to say no or say go. The net result? Rather than risking burnout, following God's permission will protect your sense of balance and leave you with a restorative sense of peace.

5 God-given happiness is a restorative reward you can experience now.

Jesus told a parable about a master who distributed money (talents)to his servants in varying amounts and told them to do something productive with the money.[7]

The most quoted line in that parable occurs when the master returns for an accounting and says to each of the two productive servants, "Well done good and faithful servant... Come and share your master's happiness."[8]

Most often the master's response is interpreted as something God will say to His servants as He rewards them with entrance into heaven and eternal bliss. Undoubted that will be true, but that is not the only or best way to interpret this parable.

Why? Because the master also says, "You have been faithful with a few things, I will put you in charge of many things." In other words this parable applies to a period of time when there's still more work to be done. That time is now.[9] Therefore, the sense of "well done"and the offer of divine happiness happens now, too.

• • • • • • • • • • • • •

So the consistent promise in the word of God is that hard work in the master's service done with the guidance and strength of the Lord is paradoxically the best way to find rest and reward now.

[7] Matthew 25:14ff   [8] Matthew 25:21,23   [9] John 9:4

Appendix A
How Saved Can You Get?

In early 2006 former ABC news anchor Bob Woodruff was nearly killed by a roadside bomb while he was on assignment covering the Iraq war.

Hundreds of rocks and pieces of metal tore through his head. A one inch rock shot through his neck missing his artery by one millimeter. The fast acting response of the army medical teams saved his life. Within the first hour they had cut away a 5x5 inch chunk of his skull to relieve pressure on his brain which swelled and protruded out into the open air. And then he lay for more than 30 days in a coma.

Everyday his wife, children and extended family waited. Hoping. Wondering.

- Would Bob ever be normal again?
- Would he regain his faculties?
- Would he ever walk and talk?
- Would he ever resume his career?
- His loving wife wondered, *Will he love me?*

The prognosis was not good.

Once Bob's physical life was saved, then all of the sudden the most important question on everybody's mind was, "How saved is he?"

As I watched his story being told on the occasion of his miraculous return to broadcast news thirteen months later, it occurred to me that the dominant question everyone was asking with baited breath—how saved will he get?—is exactly the question that Christians have wondered and debated over for centuries. Once you get saved from sin, exactly how saved can you get?

Centuries ago a mega roadside bomb of sin blasted into God's creation and tore through the human soul, killing our natural capacity to know and relate to God. We were left spiritually blind and deaf.

Our spiritual minds were knocked unconscious of our source of everything good: truth, love, peace, and eternal life.

Broken and twisted, our souls turned inward and we became self-centered in life. Our pain and suffering left us caring only about comfort and relief. Our relationships became bent strongly in the direction of needing people for what they give us rather than what we could give them.

Only a weak pulse of life remained in us. The vital signs of God's image in us barely registered. Our spiritual eyes were rolled back; we were nearly unresponsive. And yet, there was still hope. God, Himself, came and sat by our bedside, and spoke truth into our minds even while we were in a spiritual coma.

All people who hear His voice have a chance to rouse up and waken, if we do not harden our hearts. We can say, "Yes, I hear you Lord Jesus. Save me." And in that moment, in that very moment, our vital signs start to return. And we become alive to God.

But then the big question is, *how saved can we get?* How much of our hearing and speech abilities will we regain? Will our hearts ever be as strong with love as God originally created them to be? How well will we be able to see?

You see, one way to understand salvation is this: the recovery of our full capacity as human beings living in right relationship with God.

And the question is, from the moment we first receive Jesus Christ's offer of salvation, how far can we recover in this life from the devastating damage of sin? How saved can we get?

- Will we be saved, but still partially paralyzed in life, barely able to move in love, peace and joy?
- Will we be alive spiritually, but have ears that still cannot hear?

How saved can we get? Most of us have been told, "Not very."

Many Christian thinkers and teachers have concluded that we can't hope for very much. Ever since the first blast, we became so riddled with sin that nothing can separate us from the sin in us during this life. We are now as vile as the bomb itself. We will always be controlled by the sin nature until we die.

Others say that the contamination, the fragments and the damage of sin will still remain lodged in us causing us to be prone to stumbling. But we can learn to walk in holiness with the help of crutches using godly techniques to battle and restrain evil impulses, and keep us upright.

Still others, far fewer, say that we can be perfected in this life. We can fully recover the full faculties of love for God and people.

Here's what we say. We hold with the last option. If God created humankind for perfection on earth, then why would His work of salvation only bring about perfection in heaven?

So which is it? How saved can you get? The Bible says, you will experience as much salvation as you believe in.

Over and over again in Jesus' life on earth he made it abundantly clear that the operative element in what we experience of His power is our faith. He said…

- *To the blindman Bartemaus:*

    "What do you want me to do for you?" Jesus asked him.

    The blind man said, "Rabbi, I want to see."

    "Go," said Jesus, "your faith has healed you." Immediately he received his sight and followed Jesus along the road.

    Mark 10:51-52

- *To the woman with the serious hemorrhaging of blood:*

    Just then a woman who had been subject to bleeding for twelve years came up behind him and touched the edge of his cloak. She said to herself, "If I only touch his cloak, I will be healed."

    Jesus turned and saw her. "Take heart, daughter," he said, "your faith has healed you." And the woman was healed from that moment.

    Matthew 9:20-22

- *To the two blind men:*

    The blind men came to him, and he asked them, "Do you believe that I am able to do this?"

    "Yes, Lord," they replied.

    Then he touched their eyes and said, "According to your faith will it be done to you"; and their sight was restored.

    Matthew 9:28-30

- *To the Canaanite woman whose daughter was suffering from demon-possession:*

A Canaanite woman from that vicinity came to him, crying out, "Lord, Son of David, have mercy on me! My daughter is suffering terribly from demon-possession."

Jesus did not answer a word. So his disciples came to him and urged him, "Send her away, for she keeps crying out after us."

He answered, "I was sent only to the lost sheep of Israel."

The woman came and knelt before him. "Lord, help me!" she said.

He replied, "It is not right to take the children's bread and toss it to their dogs."

"Yes, Lord," she said, "but even the dogs eat the crumbs that fall from their masters' table."

Then Jesus answered, "Woman, you have great faith! Your request is granted." And her daughter was healed from that very hour.

Matthew 15:22-28

- *To the centurion with a terminally ill servant:*

When Jesus had entered Capernaum, a centurion came to him, asking for help. "Lord," he said, "my servant lies at home paralyzed and in terrible suffering."

Jesus said to him, "I will go and heal him."

The centurion replied, "Lord, I do not deserve to have you come under my roof. But just say the word, and my servant will be healed. For I myself am a man under authority, with soldiers under me. I tell this one, 'Go,' and he goes; and that one, 'Come,' and he comes. I say to my servant, 'Do this,' and he does it."

When Jesus heard this, he was astonished and said to those following him, "I tell you the truth, I have not found anyone in Israel with such great faith.

Then Jesus said to the centurion, "Go! It will be done just as you believed it would." And his servant was healed at that very hour.

Matthew 8:5-13

And I could go on and remind you of:
- times Jesus expected His disciples to exercise faith;
- times when he urged them to believe in what was possible with faith even as small as a mustard seed;
- the time Jesus visited His own home town where He could do so little because of the absence of faith.

What is it about this principle that we don't understand? Why do we excuse our unbelief and justify it in sophisticated doctrines?

How saved can you get? Here's the simple truth: *you experience as much salvation as you believe in.*

From the moment you and I are first saved, we are like Bob Woodruff waking up from a coma. From that point on he had to learn to speak, to walk, to think, to relate. He was surrounded by people who patiently loved him and helped him regain nearly all the abilities that he once had.

In the same way, as we are surrounded by fellow believers and loving support we can regain the abilities we humans were first created to have.

- Slowly we can learn to walk as Jesus walked.
- We can learn to hear and understand God,

and speak to Him as we regain our spiritual communication ability.
- We can see the world and other people as they were meant to be seen.
- Even the glory of God in the universe itself will become apparent to us.
- We can successfully perform the work God designed us to do.

That's how saved we can get! Full salvation. But if full salvation is ever to occur here are five keys:
- Believe in full recovery and employ faith-filled proclamation
- Live under the influence of true believers—people who believe in the possibility of full recovery.
- Work hard in therapy. (e.g., soaking in and exercising faith in the Word of God and prayer)
- Keep believing despite contrary evidence.
- Keep your eyes fixed on Jesus as your example. Or else you start to sink into the waves of doubt and contrary evidence.

Yes, Jesus is our prime example. He came not only to show us what God is like, but also what man can be like when living in right relation to God. He is the picture of how saved you can get. Therefore you can look at Him and say, "That's how saved I want to be."

Appendix B
Healing Today?

There are several paradigms for salvation. A paradigm is a "way of seeing" something complex from one particular angle. For instance, the meaning of the cross of Jesus Christ is far greater than what any one paradigm can explain.

The modern evangelical paradigm for salvation is the **courtroom (judicial) paradigm**, i.e. people are *guilty* of sin and rebellion against God, *sentenced* to eternal death, but Jesus suffered that penalty on our behalf and those who believe in Him are *pardoned*.

Another less popular but equally biblical salvation paradigm is the **healing (therapeutic) paradigm**, i.e. God offers *healing* and *restoration* to people who are *wounded* and *broken* by the *disease* of sin.

This paradigm deserves more attention as a basis for faith, hope and ministry.

In John 3:14-16 Jesus identifies his work on the cross with an episode in the Old Testament when the people of Israel were bitten by snakes as punishment for their complaining against God. He said:

> *Just as Moses lifted up the snake in the desert, so the Son of Man must be lifted up, that everyone who believes in him may have eternal life. For God so loved the world that he gave his one and only Son, that whoever believes in him shall not perish but have eternal life.*

Here's how that Old Testament episode goes:

> *[The people of Israel] traveled from Mount Hor along the route to the Red Sea, to go around Edom. But the people grew impatient on the way; they spoke against God and against Moses, and said, "Why have you brought us up out of Egypt to die in the desert? There is no bread! There is no water! And we detest this miserable food!"*
>
> *Then the LORD sent venomous snakes among them; they bit the people and many Israelites died. The people came to Moses and said, "We sinned when we spoke against the LORD and against you. Pray that the LORD will take the snakes away from us." So Moses prayed for the people.*
>
> *The LORD said to Moses, "Make a snake and put it up on a pole; anyone who is bitten can look at it and live." So Moses made a bronze snake and put it up on a pole. Then when anyone was bitten by a snake and looked at the bronze snake, he lived.*
>
> Numbers 21: 4-9

This story introduces us to two very important principles of salvation that recur over and over again in the Bible.

First, **the effect of sin is always suffering.** It may happen as a natural course of events. Or it may occur by God's direct involvement by either His removing protection, or His inflicting disease.

All sin causes suffering.

But to say all sin causes suffering does not mean all suffering is caused by sin. That's faulty logic. All healthy dogs may have four legs, but not all animals that have four legs are dogs.

The second principle we learn from this episode is that **God makes a way for sin-based suffering to cease through the exercise of faith.**

So when Jesus connects His death on the cross with this O.T. episode, He is clearly invoking both principles: namely, the remedy for the harmful consequences of sin is available for anyone who will place His faith in Jesus.

In other words, here we have a strong of example of this other salvation paradigm that shows up throughout scripture: the healing paradigm. Salvation is about being restored to wholeness, health, stability, harmony of function and design. It is a remedy for disease, disequilibrium, brokenness, disintegration, disharmony and dysfunction.

In fact, the verb commonly translated "to save" (sozo) is used 16 times in the New Testament in situations of healing. One classic example is in the case of the woman who was hemorrhaging blood for 12 years. When she boldly pushed her way through the crowd just to touch the hem of Jesus garment,

> She said to herself, "If I only touch his cloak, I will be healed."
> Jesus turned and saw her. "Take heart, daughter," he said, "your faith has **healed** you." And the woman was healed from that moment.
> Matthew 9:21-22

Here are some other examples where the verb "to save" is used for healing.

> When they had crossed over, they landed at Gennesaret. And when the men of that place recognized Jesus, they sent word to all the surrounding country. People brought all their sick to him and begged him to let the sick just touch the edge of his cloak, and all who touched him were **healed**.
> Matthew 14:34-36

> Then one of the synagogue rulers, named Jairus, came there. Seeing Jesus, he fell at his feet and pleaded earnestly with him, "My little daughter is dying. Please come and put your hands on her so that she will be **healed** and live."
> Mark 5:22-23

> "What do you want me to do for you?" Jesus asked him.
> The blind man said, "Rabbi, I want to see."
> "Go," said Jesus, "your faith has **healed** you." Immediately he received his sight and followed Jesus along the road.
> Mark 10:51-52

> They had Peter and John brought before them and began to question them: "By what power or what name did you do this?"
> Then Peter, filled with the Holy Spirit, said to them: "Rulers and elders of the people! If we are being called to account today for an act of kindness shown to a cripple and are asked how he was **healed**, then know this, you and all the people of Israel: It is by the name of Jesus Christ of Nazareth, whom you cruci-

*fied but whom God raised from the dead, that this man stands before you **healed**.*
Acts 4:7-10

Interesting how this word for salvation and the word for healing are so often one and the same. Is it possible that we should see salvation through the lens of healing in more than just a figurative sense?

Yes. But now here's the million dollar question: How far do we go with this healing paradigm? Did Jesus' death on the cross bring only a remedy for the death problem – or did it also bring a remedy for other suffering problems brought on by sin?

For generations there have been biblical theologians who have argued for the fact of healing found in Jesus' work on the cross, often spoken of as *healing in the atonement.*

They use a Messianic text like Isaiah 52-53 to support that claim.

> *See, my servant will act wisely; he will be raised and lifted up and highly exalted. His appearance was so disfigured beyond that of any man and his form marred beyond human likeness. He had no beauty or majesty to attract us to him, nothing in his appearance that we should desire him.*
>
> *He was despised and rejected by men, a man of sorrows, and familiar with suffering. Surely he took up our infirmities and carried our sorrows. But he was pierced for our transgressions; he was crushed for our iniquities; the punishment that brought us peace was upon him, and by his wounds we are healed.*
Isaiah 52:13-53:5

For years I argued against this viewpoint. I interpreted this text to be referring only to *soul sickness.* But I have been won over for several reasons:

◆ The preponderance of Jesus' ministry was healing-centered. Why would His compassion overflow in this way during His earthly ministry and then cease to overflow like this when He returned to heaven? No one could answer that question satisfactorily for me.

◆ Jesus connected physical healing with spiritual healing. In other words we may separate them, but Jesus related to human need as if the spiritual and physical were cut from the same cloth. For example, he said to the paralytic in Matthew 9:6: *But so that you may know that the Son of Man has authority on earth to forgive sins... ." Then he said to the paralytic, "Get up, take your mat and go home."*

◆ He identified His acts of physical healing with the nature of the kingdom not just proof of the kingdom. For example, when John the baptist started having doubts about Jesus identity, he sent someone to ask Jesus if He was the Messiah. Jesus' reply in Luke 7:20-23 is very striking:

> *When the men came to Jesus, they said, "John the Baptist sent us to you to ask, 'Are you the one who was to come, or should we expect someone else?'"*
>
> *At that very time Jesus cured many who had diseases, sicknesses and evil spirits, and gave sight to many who were blind. So he replied to the messengers, "Go back and report to John what you have seen and heard: The blind receive sight, the lame walk, those who have leprosy are cured, the*

deaf hear, the dead are raised, and the good news is preached to the poor. Blessed is the man who does not fall away on account of me."

◆Finally, if we truly believe that the Word of God is inspired by the Holy Spirit, here's the crowning proof. The apostle Matthew—guided by the Holy Spirit—used Isaiah 53 to explain the meaning of Jesus' healing ministries in Matthew 8:16-17. *When evening came, many who were demon-possessed were brought to him, and he drove out the spirits with a word and healed all the sick. This was to fulfill what was spoken through the prophet Isaiah: "He took up our infirmities and carried our diseases."*
Remember, Matthew was writing His gospel long after Jesus' death, and by this time the early church was beginning to piece together its theology of the cross.

When we marshal this amount of evidence, it seems undeniable that salvation means *God makes a way for sin-based suffering to cease through exercising faith in Jesus' work on the cross.*

Even with this biblical evidence people have argued against miraculous healing being normative as opposed to exceptional. Let's take a look at those arguments. Due to my own track record, I have come to see these arguments as highly prejudiced. That is, like me, people are out to disprove something they have already decided cannot be possible.

Argument #1: ***The miracles of healing were only temporarily commonplace for the purpose of establishing the early church.*** This might be called the "leading edge theory." The argument is made that as the gospel first spread from Jerusalem outward to Judea and Samaria, and then to farther parts of the world, powerful signs accompanied that first wave, that *leading edge* so to speak, as a way of confirming the gospel message. But then, once the gospel took root, things settled down, and those miraculous proofs were no longer necessary.

Is this theory valid? How long do these miraculous signs need to continue beyond those "leading edge" days in order to be considered normative?

◆Nearly 30 years after Pentecost, well after the gospel had reached all the way to Rome, back home at "headquarters" in the mother church in Jerusalem, apparently the ministry of miraculous healing continued on as the norm. For that is when the great church leader James, known for his stability and wisdom wrote:
Is any one of you sick? He should call the elders of the church to pray over him and anoint him with oil in the name of the Lord. And the prayer offered in faith will make the sick person well; the Lord will raise him up. If he has sinned, he will be forgiven. Therefore confess your sins to each other and pray for each other so that you may be healed. The prayer of a righteous man is powerful and effective.   James 5:13-16

◆Then listen to these words from Mark 16:15-18. *He said to them, "Go into all the world and preach the good news to all creation. Whoever believes and is baptized will be saved... And these signs will accompany those who believe: In my name they will drive out demons; they will speak in new tongues; they will pick up snakes with their hands; and when they drink deadly poison, it will not hurt them at all; they will place their hands on sick people, and they will get well."* It does not say these signs will accompany those who go out and preach; it says the signs "will accompany those who believe."

Now you may know enough to argue that this portion of Mark's gospel has been highly questioned as not being in his original manuscript. In fact your Bible may even say in the footnotes: "The most reliable early manuscripts and other ancient witnesses do not have Mark 16:9-20."

People have used that as an excuse to toss it out as support for signs and wonders. When as a matter of fact the addition of these verses is actually remarkable proof for the continuation of the signs and wonders. Why? Because scholars have pinpointed this addition to the original text to have been inserted somewhere around the year A.D. 125. That means nearly 100 years after Pentecost someone felt like it was important enough to make this point that it was added. And… And!... The content of this addition was accepted as so valid that it apparently became the accepted popular rendition of the gospel from then on. That means the content must have conformed so well to reality that it was not considered spurious or crackpot. This is strong evidence that signs and wonders were expected to be commonplace even into the second century of the church—well beyond the initial missionary expansion decades.

But then here's another argument.

Argument #2: *There is little historical evidence of signs and wonders being commonplace throughout church history.* In other words, if healing and miracles were normative, church history would have a lot more evidence. Question: Since when do we deduce what is possible from what is common? The fact that most Americans do not experience financial freedom and are in credit card debt up to their eyeballs does not prove that it is not possible to have savings accounts. If church history teaches anything it teaches that people live well below the norms of the kingdom in every respect. Church history has never been an accurate reflection of what is normative in the city of God. It is more a reflection of what is deficient in the city of man.

Argument #3: *Modern medicine makes healing miracles no longer necessary.* This only seems to make sense until you look at all that the medical arts cannot heal. Praise God for what doctors can accomplish. But try telling a blind person, therefore, we don't need miracles of healing anymore.

In summary, the Lord has taken my prejudiced mind and completely changed my belief system. He did this not primarily by exposing me to case after case of miraculous healing, but just by using evidence in the word of God.

When you begin to look at scripture with the healing paradigm, you begin to see it everywhere in all sorts of forms. God saves spiritually, physically, psychologically (sound mind), relationally (reconciliation, forgiveness, peace and justice), and materially (poverty to prosperity, abundant crops).

Salvation is healing, and we should expect to see healing occur much more frequently than we do, because healing is a function of God's unchanging nature of love and central to His work on the cross.

However, we must be very careful as we apply this doctrine. People who properly believe in the possibility of extensive healing today may have an unfortunate tendency to go too far.

Five Guardrails About Healing

Let's lay down some guard rails, because not all sickness gets healed. And we certainly do not want to spawn the over-enthusiastic and damaging idea, that if you don't get healed, you just didn't have enough faith.

1) *Not all suffering is due to sin.* The whole Old Testament book of Job makes that point. Paul's thorn in the flesh provides New Testament corroboration to this fact (2 Corinthians 12:7-10).

2) *Jesus places a higher priority on your soul health than your physical health,* even to the degree that he "advocated" disabling yourself if that meant greater likelihood of holiness. (I.e. "If your hand causes you to sin cut it off…" Matthew 5:30) Therefore, some suffering may be therapy for the soul. God knows when that is the case. We don't. The most we can say is: *Lord, if this suffering or circumstance serves to heal my soul, then so be it.*

3) *Jesus places a higher priority on what it takes to save others.* Your suffering may be strategic in bringing others to faith. Chronic suffering (a la quadraplegic Joni Tada) may be spiritually beneficial to others. So, again, the most you can say is: *Lord, if my suffering serves to heal or save others, then so be it.*

4) *Some suffering cannot be healed until a root cause is first corrected.* Often times there are spiritual causes to physical problems. Did you know for example that there are scores of testimonies to a connection between unforgiveness, bitterness and arthritic symptoms? That doesn't mean that that connection is always or even often the case, but it can be. Those who engage in healing ministries see it often enough to explore that question.

5) *Timing and method must bring the most glory to Jesus.* Even if a disability or sickness is eligible for healing (i.e. something God wants to heal and is "allowed" to heal by the conditions of His own kingdom laws) He will (and must be allowed to) perform that healing in a way and at a time that brings the most glory to Him. For example, the blind man in John 9 was allowed to live for years in blindness before the time was right for his healing.

With those guardrails set carefully in place, we unequivocally make this affirmation: **Miracles of healing should be happening more as the rule rather than the exception as we continue to exercise faith in the cross of Jesus Christ.**

If we disciples of Jesus would believe this and grow in active faith we would wind up growing in our love for God as we stand amazed at how He pours out grace lavishly!

Appendix C
Behind the Closed Door

Look at the adjacent diagram. You will see three columns labeled *sub-standard*, *standard* and *surpassing* ministries.

Our belief is that true holiness (i.e. godliness) is love in action with moral perfection. That means love is being offered in such a way that the best possible help and conditions for another person's well-being are made available.

Therefore, to pursue holiness requires that we pursue every available resource, spiritual gift, and counsel so that we offer people the most help possible. Anything less than offering the most we can is less than godly love.

Yet sadly, God's people far too often rule out the best resources and abilities available—those that come directly from the Holy Spirit.

Take some time examining the diagram and simple explanations for each column. See if you don't agree the Christ's love compels us to re-open the "surpassing ministries" door if we've let it close.

SUB-STANDARD MINISTRIES

Efforts guided by skilled practitioners.

Preaching
Teaching
Testimony
Prayer
Worship services
Acts of service
Evangelistic work
Blessing

EXPLANATION: It is a natural tendency to rely on human experience and wisdom whenever we want to succeed in any important enterprise. Ministry pursuits are no different. So we read books, attend seminars, and consult the experts to learn and practice methods that others have found successful. There is nothing wrong with this, unless of course that is the extent of our quest for effectiveness. Too often it is. We completely neglect the absolute necessity of seeking the presence and work of the Holy Spirit. As a result, our efforts and effectiveness are sub-standard.

STANDARD MINISTRIES

Efforts *anointed* by the Holy Spirit.

Preaching
Teaching
Testimony
Prayer
Worship services
Acts of service
Evangelistic work
Blessing

EXPLANATION: Notice that the list of ministry activities is exactly the same as the "sub-standard" list. The only difference is that these ministries are not engaged in without seeking the presence and empowerment of the Holy Spirit. This is what we call the "anointing." By all means, any Christian or Christian group should never employ their gifts, energies and wisdom in ministry without the anointing. It is good when they do and the Lord blesses their efforts. This is the "standard" and a proper approach to ministry. But there's even more effectiveness possible. Unfortunately, the church often closes the door to that possibility out of fear.

Danger Keep Out

SURPASSING MINISTRIES

Efforts *initiated* by the Holy Spirit.

Specific instructions
Prophetic words
Praying in the Spirit
Gifts of the Spirit
Healings
Deliverance
Impartation
Blessing
Binding; loosing

EXPLANATION: Very often effectiveness requires perfect timing, just the right words, or properly aimed supernatural power. These are things that require more than our methods and skills anointed by the Spirit. They require the initiation of the Spirit. He can prompt us with ideas and instructions to act and speak in ways that we have no way of knowing, but which are precisely what is needed in a given situation. We must not close the door to these Spirit-prompted ministries, no matter how misused they might be. We must love people with true godly love that offers the best help available.